With a Little Luck

Luck is what happens when preparation meets opportunity.

—SENECA

(Roman author who lived from about 4 B.C. to A.D. 65)

Contents

With a Little Luck

Introduction:

Off to Serendip

Everyone knows that in 1492 Columbus sailed the ocean blue and landed in the Americas. What is often forgotten is that the great explorer wasn't *looking* for the Americas at all on his famous voyage. He was searching for a new sea route to Asia and only bumped into the New World because it blocked his path. Although Christopher Columbus wasn't the first European to arrive there, his unexpected arrival in the Americas opened the region to European settlement.

One day in the mid-1900s, after Swiss inventor Georges de Mestral had walked his dog, he noticed that his clothing and his dog were covered with cockleburs. Curious about these plants, de Mestral studied cockleburs under a microscope and discovered that their hooked prickles made them stick to things. This led to his inventing a new kind of fastener that had hooks on one side and loops on the other. De Mestral's creation became known as Velcro.

Columbus's arrival in the New World and the invention of Velcro are examples of what many people call *serendipity*. This word, which has become popular in recent years, actually goes back a long way. Centuries ago a fairy tale was told in Persia (today Iran) called *The Three Princes of Serendip*, whose heroes continually made unexpected discoveries through good fortune and their own cleverness. In 1754 the English author Horace Walpole took the name Serendip and coined the word *serendipity*, meaning to make an unexpected discovery or breakthrough by accident.

All of the discoveries in this book are serendipitous in one way or another. A young girl in Spain explores a cave that happens to contain a number of ancient and priceless paintings. A Connecticut man accidentally drops some rubber onto a hot stove and discovers the process that launches the rubber industry. An English scientist observes an apple fall from a tree and suddenly understands what keeps the moon and the planets in their orbits.

Yet none of these advances was the result of luck alone. Her intense curiosity led the Spanish girl to explore the dark cave. The Connecticut man experimented with rubber for years before the accident helped him discover how to process rubber. The English scientist had been pondering the question of how the universe is held together long before the falling apple inspired him.

Alexander Fleming, the discoverer of penicillin (see Chapter vii) resented it when people asserted that his breakthrough was merely the result of blind luck. While luck often plays a role in discoveries, admitted Fleming, the trick is to be observant enough to take advantage of a serendipitous occurrence. Advising would-be discoverers to stay on the lookout for the unexpected, Fleming said, "All of us, in our ordinary pursuits, can do valuable research, by continual and critical observation. If something unusual happens, we should think about it and try to find out what it means."

Isaac Newton

Isaac Newton i

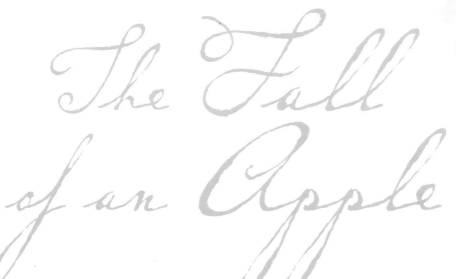

The Fall of an Apple

How is the universe put together? People have wondered about that from the time our prehistoric ancestors first looked up at the night sky.

The ancient Egyptians believed that their goddess of the heavens, Nut, had stars covering her body. At night Nut stretched across our world, touching the ground only with her fingertips and toes at the horizons. As each night ended, Nut gave birth to the sun, which during the daylight hours glided across her back in a barge.

The Babylonians, who lived near the Tigris and Euphrates rivers in what is now Iraq, believed that Earth was a flat disk surrounded by water, and that the heavens were a starry dome held up by mountains. Noting that rain fell from someplace high in the sky, the Babylonians concluded that another vast body of water lay above the dome of stars.

Although a few ancient Greek astronomers insisted that the heavenly bodies were large and separated by vast spaces, they were considered oddballs. The Greek astronomer Ptolemy (about A.D. 100–about A.D. 165) became known as the greatest ancient authority on the construction of the universe. Unfortunately, his basic ideas were completely wrong. Earth, claimed Ptolemy, was a special body that stood completely motionless at the center of the universe. The moon, the sun, and the planets all orbited our world at various speeds. Furthermore, he asserted, the stars were nothing more than bright points of light twinkling on a giant dome that rotated above Earth each night.

The "Ptolemaic System," as it became known, reigned supreme for nearly fourteen centuries. Not until the 1500s was there a major challenge to Ptolemy's idea of the Earth-centered universe.

That challenge came from a Polish astronomer, Nicolaus Copernicus (1473–1543). Based on certain planetary movements, Copernicus rejected the idea that Earth was a special body at the center of everything. In his book *On the Revolutions of the Heavenly Spheres*, which was published the year he died, Copernicus described the true nature of the heavens. Earth is a planet—one of several large bodies orbiting the sun. The only reason celestial objects appear to circle above us is that our planet spins like a top. One body, the moon, actually does orbit Earth, Copernicus realized, but at the same time it and Earth orbit the sun together.

The "Copernican System" was accurate, yet at first most astronomers rejected the concept. The Italian astronomer Galileo Galilei (1564–1642) was an exception. During the winter of 1609–1610, Galileo became the first scientist to make astronomical discoveries with a telescope. He saw that the moon was a large globe covered by mountains and craters, and observed the brilliant white planet, Venus; the giant planet, Jupiter; and the ringed planet, Saturn. Perhaps the most astonishing sight was that at least four moons orbited Jupiter. Here was proof that at least some heavenly bodies *didn't* orbit our Earth. Besides all this, Galileo saw that the Milky Way was made up of stars "so numerous as to be almost beyond belief." Either the dome with the little stars on it was more crowded than Ptolemy had thought, or, more likely, there was no dome and the sky was filled with millions of stars at varying distances.

The German astronomer Johannes Kepler (1571–1630) also embraced the Copernican System. Kepler made several major discoveries about planetary motions. One was that the planets do not orbit the sun in perfectly circular paths. Instead, their orbits are elliptical, or egg-shaped.

Still, the year 1600 came and went, as did the year 1650, and the Copernican System didn't yet have many followers. To nearly everyone, the Ptolemaic System made more sense. It really *did* appear that the heavenly bodies moved in circles above our motionless Earth. Besides, the Copernican System left some crucial questions unanswered. If all the planets were big worlds orbiting the sun, what kept them from flying off into space? What kept the moon from slipping away from Earth? And if our Earth moved around the sun and spun continuously, why didn't we get flung off its surface?

Johannes Kepler tackled one of these questions. He concluded that the sun shot out some kind of mysterious rays that held the planets in their orbits. But scientists would have to do better than *that* for the Copernican System to seem plausible.

Early on Christmas morning of 1642, on a farm in the hamlet of Woolsthorpe, England, a baby was born who would one day answer these questions. The boy's father had died several weeks before his birth. Hannah Newton, the baby's mother, named him Isaac. Many stories were handed down about how small and frail Isaac was as an infant. His mother later told Isaac that at birth he might have fit into a quart pot. Just so that he could hold up his head, his neck had to be fitted with a kind of collar. It was also said that two women sent to bring medicine for baby Isaac took their time, certain that he couldn't possibly still be alive upon their return. But little Isaac fooled them and eventually lived far beyond infancy.

In the 1600s, widows were expected to remarry quickly, for they had little opportunity to support themselves and their children. When Isaac was three years old, his mother married a wealthy, elderly clergyman named Barnabas Smith. Hannah Newton Smith moved into her new husband's home in a nearby town, leaving Isaac in the care of her own mother, Isaac's grandmother, at Woolsthorpe. Hannah provided for her son, insisting that her new husband remodel the Newton home in Woolsthorpe, which was one day to go to Isaac. But three-year-old Isaac didn't understand or care that his mother was doing her best for him. Having never seen his father, he was now deprived of his mother, too. For a few years, he seems to have seen her only occasionally. He was so resentful that, in one of his early writings, Isaac confessed to "threatening my father and mother Smith to burn them and the house over them."

Isaac wasn't much of a student. Instead of studying his schoolwork, he preferred to play by himself, draw, and build and invent things.

As a child, Isaac attended two different schools near Woolsthorpe where he learned reading, writing, and arithmetic. For quite a while he wasn't much of a student. Instead of studying his schoolwork, he preferred to play by himself, draw, and build and invent things.

He built sundials—devices that keep time by measuring the changing angle of the sun's shadow—including two sundials he carved on the side of his house at Woolsthorpe. He put together a model windmill. On windless days, Isaac powered his miniature mill with a pet mouse he called "the miller," who set the device in motion by chasing bits of corn. Isaac also loved to build kites. In those days, many people were terrified of comets, which were believed to be omens of coming disasters. Isaac attached lanterns to the tails of sturdy kites and flew them at night. He thought it was a great joke when his neighbors spotted one of his illuminated kites in the sky and spread the alarm about the new comet. Another of his childhood inventions was a four-wheeled carriage that the driver operated by turning a handle from inside the little vehicle. It may have been the first toy car ever constructed.

At the age of twelve, Isaac was sent off to King's School at Grantham, about six miles from Woolsthorpe. Because of the school's distance from home, his mother arranged for Isaac to board with an apothecary (what we would call a pharmacist) named Mr. Clark. Isaac enjoyed living at the Clarks'. He must have had quite a time helping Mr. Clark mix medicines, for in those days it was believed that the more foul-tasting the concoction, the better its chances to drive off disease. For his living space, Isaac was

The house in Woolsthorpe, England, where Isaac Newton was born; the sundials he made as a child are visible on a side wall.

given the Clarks' attic. He covered its walls with mathematical diagrams as well as with pictures he drew and framed of famous people, birds and other animals, and sailing vessels. But it took a kick in the stomach for Isaac to start applying himself at King's School.

The students at the school were ranked according to their academic achievements. Isaac quickly sank to the bottom, ranking next to last in a class of nearly a hundred students. One day as the students headed to school, the boy who ranked just ahead of him gave him an unexpected and painful kick. Infuriated, Isaac challenged the boy to meet him in the churchyard at the end of the day. The two fought, and Isaac won, but afterward someone reminded Isaac that the vanquished boy still stood above him in school. Isaac began concentrating on his studies so intensely that he gradually rose to the top position in his class.

Meanwhile, Isaac's stepfather, Barnabas Smith, had died and his mother had returned to Woolsthorpe. Accompanying her were two sons and a daughter that she had had with Smith. When Isaac was about fifteen, his mother informed him that his school days were over. The time had come for him to return home and help run the farm.

Isaac, who had grown to love school, was furious. He returned home as ordered but refused to do farm chores. Instead of working in the fields, he sat under a tree reading a book, or building wooden models with his tools. Instead of tending the sheep, he allowed them to wander onto a neighbor's property, causing damage that his mother had to pay for. When his mother sent Isaac to Grantham on Saturday mornings to sell the family's crops and buy supplies, he neglected his tasks and went to his old room in the Clarks' attic to read. Finally Henry Stokes, the King's School headmaster (what we would call the principal), decided to speak out for the youth who had risen from the bottom to the top of his class. Mr. Stokes visited Isaac's mother and informed her that her son had a brilliant scientific mind. He convinced her that Isaac should complete his studies at King's School and then go on to the university.

Around the time that Isaac returned to school he performed one of his first scientific experiments. On a calm day, Isaac jumped as far as he could and measured the distance. Then, during a powerful storm, he jumped first with the wind at his back, then against the wind. He could jump considerably farther with the wind's help, he found. He then invented a formula to measure the force of a storm based on how far he could jump with and against the wind.

When asked how he had made his many discoveries, Newton said, "I keep the subject constantly before me."

After finishing up at King's School, eighteen-year-old Isaac entered Cambridge University in 1661. He enrolled as a sizar—a student who paid his way through college by waiting tables, running errands, and doing odd jobs. He didn't do very well in college, probably because he spent so much time studying mathematics and astronomy. He read Nicolaus Copernicus's work and became convinced that Earth orbited the sun, as the Polish astronomer had claimed. He also read the writings of Johannes Kepler, who declared that some mysterious rays bound the planets in their orbits, and of Galileo, who had observed the heavens with his telescope.

Isaac didn't have a telescope yet, but he began making naked-eye observations of the sky. He observed a comet in late 1664, and another in the spring of 1665. He gazed at the moon and the planets by night, and hurt his eyes looking at the sun in a mirror by day. Isaac wondered: What kept the moon orbiting Earth, and Earth and the other planets orbiting the sun?

In the spring of 1665, at the age of twenty-two, Isaac Newton received his bachelor's degree from Cambridge University. He graduated without special distinction. He was planning to continue at Cambridge in pursuit of his master's degree when England suffered a severe outbreak of bubonic plague—a disease caused by bacteria transferred from rats to people by fleas. In the summer of 1665 the plague killed more than a tenth of the people in London. Among other places in England, Cambridge University was abandoned and wouldn't reopen until the spring of 1667. Isaac spent that year and a half on the family farm in Woolsthorpe.

Later in life, when asked how he had made his many discoveries, Newton said, "I keep the subject constantly before me." He meant that when working on a scientific problem he had a one-track mind. Many stories were told about Newton forgetting to eat or put on his clothes when immersed in research. He must have often gone hungry and undressed during his year and a half at Woolsthorpe, for during that time he made three of the greatest scientific discoveries in history.

During this period Newton discovered a new branch of mathematics called *calculus*. The German mathematician Gottfried Leibniz is also credited with discovering calculus at about the same time. Today calculus is an extremely important scientific tool. Physicists and astronomers use it to solve problems in which the quantities involved do not remain constant.

Newton also experimented with light and color. Using a triangular glass called a *prism*, he found that sunlight was actually made up of a variety of colors. He named the rainbow of colors produced by the prism the *spectrum*—Latin for "ghost." Today astronomers study spectra of stars to learn about their chemical composition, temperature, and speed and direction of movement.

But it was his third discovery that shook the world. For several years Newton had been thinking about the force that kept the moon and planets in orbit. In the autumn of 1665 or 1666, he was sitting in the orchard at his home in Woolsthorpe deep in thought when he noticed an apple fall

The fall of the apple inspired Newton to conclude that . . .

from the branch of a tree to the ground. Isaac Newton had a sudden flash of inspiration: The same force that pulled the apple to the ground also kept the planets in their orbits around the sun and the moon in orbit around Earth. Newton then figured out many details of how this force works. The force was named *gravitation* or *gravity*, from the Latin word *gravis*, meaning "heavy."

It is often implied that, without the fall of the apple, Isaac Newton wouldn't have had his insights about gravitation. The truth is, because of the way he dwelled on a subject, he was ripe to make his discovery. Had there been no falling apple, he probably would have had the same insight watching a book slip from someone's hands, or rain fall from the sky. Still, it was an apple that inspired him, and that piece of fruit, which he may have eaten, is forever linked with Newton's discoveries concerning gravitation.

In 1667 Newton returned to Cambridge as a graduate student, and two years later he became a mathematics professor at the university. The classes he taught were so difficult that at times he had no students and reportedly delivered his lectures to an empty room. Over the years, Newton continued to learn more about the nature of gravitation, yet he didn't publish a book on the subject. Why not? He was so sensitive to possible criticism that he tended to keep information to himself—much like his lecturing to the walls.

Fortunately, when Isaac entered his middle years he encountered a young English astronomer named Edmond Halley (1656–1742). Although best known for the comet named after him, Halley's greatest contribution to science was convincing Isaac Newton to write a book describing his discoveries about gravitation and motion. Halley even arranged to pay for the book's publication.

Isaac Newton's masterpiece, written in Latin, was published in 1687. Its

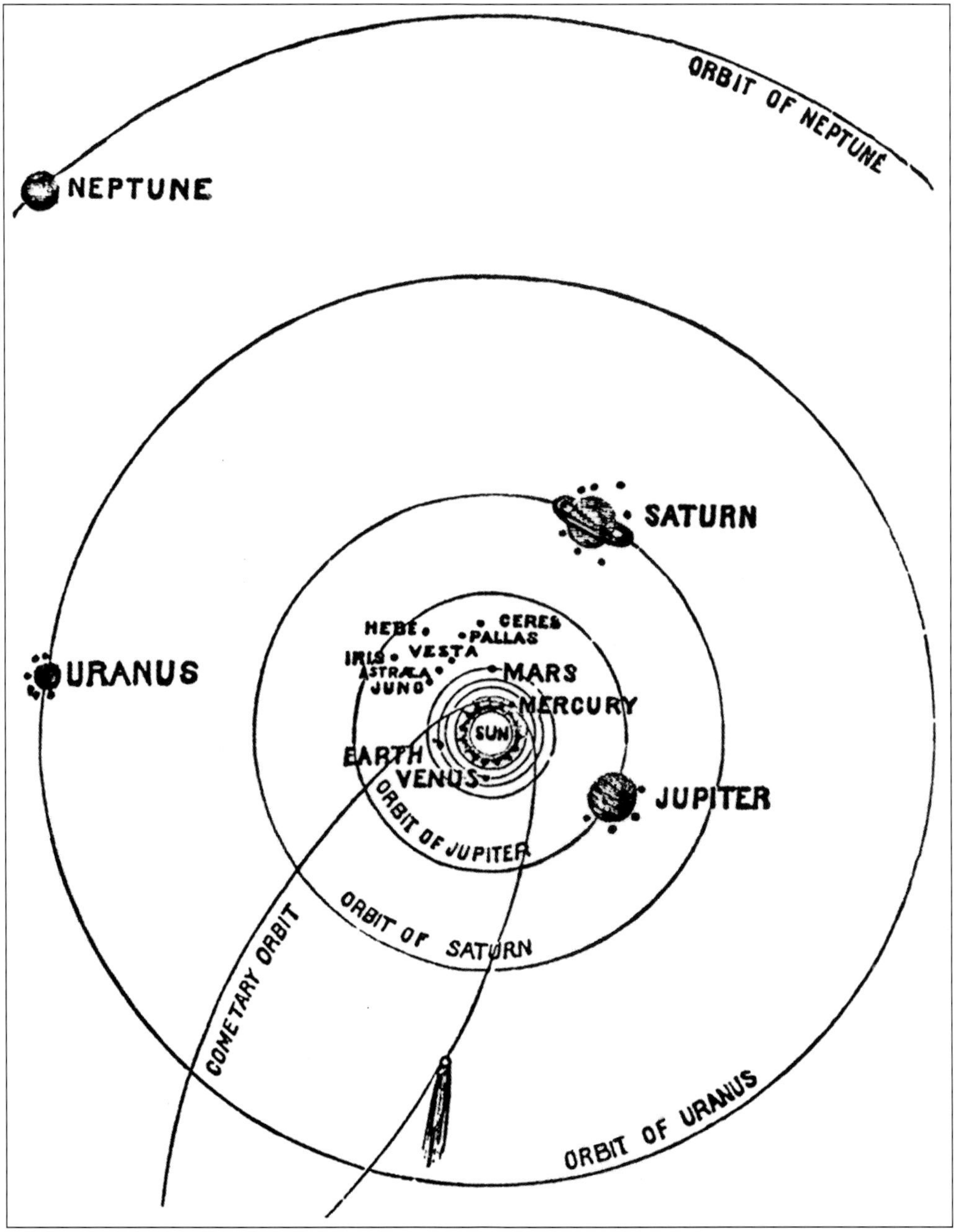

... the same force that pulled the apple to the ground (gravitation) keeps the planets in orbit around the sun and the moons in orbit around the planets. This diagram from the 1880s does not include Pluto because it hadn't yet been discovered; the objects between Mars and Jupiter are called asteroids, and the object at bottom with a tail is a comet.

title was *Philosophiae Naturalis Principia Mathematica*, which in English means *Mathematical Principles of Natural Philosophy*. Often simply called the *Principia* for short, it is widely considered to be the greatest scientific book ever written, for it describes, in detail, how gravitation and motion operate in the Copernican Universe.

"If I have seen further than others, it was because I stood upon the shoulders of giants."

No single moment marked the triumph of the Copernican System, but the *Principia* ended all serious objections to it. Thanks largely to Isaac Newton, by about the year 1700 most educated people knew that our Earth and the other planets orbit the sun, whose gravitational attraction keep them from flying off into space.

Among his other work, Newton helped develop a new kind of telescope. The earliest telescopes, called *refractors*, worked with lenses. Newton's telescope, the *reflector*, worked with mirrors. Today all of the world's largest optical telescopes are reflectors.

Newton once commented about his monumental achievements: "If I have seen further than others, it was because I stood upon the shoulders of giants." He knew that without the work of earlier scientists such as Copernicus, Galileo, and Kepler, he couldn't have accomplished all that he did. Similarly, many later scientists such as Albert Einstein have built upon Newton's work.

Isaac Newton, who never married, was cared for in his later years by his niece Catherine (his half-sister's daughter). It was said that as a very old man, Newton liked to take bubble baths. He would sit for hours in his tub, blowing soap bubbles through a pipe, and intently watching them burst. The scientific giant, who as a child hadn't been expected to live very long, died in the spring of 1727 at the age of eighty-four.

Mary Anning ii

"The Princess of Paleontology"

There are many people who find it impossible to spot an unusual object on the ground without picking it up and studying it further. Is that small metal object an old coin from a buried treasure? Is that odd-looking rock a fossil from the age of the dinosaurs? An English girl named Mary Anning was one of these people, and it led her into quite an unusual career for a young woman of the 1800s.

Mary was born in Lyme Regis, a small seaside town in southern England, on May 21, 1799. She was one of about ten children of Richard and Molly Anning, who lived in a house on Bridge Street, just fifty feet from the sea. Nearly half of all children in England died of childhood illnesses in those days. The Annings were unluckier than most, losing all of their children except Mary and her older brother Joseph. Mary herself had an extremely close call at the age of fifteen months—but not because of disease.

When Mary was a baby, her parents employed a nursemaid named Elizabeth Haskins. On August 19, 1800, Mrs. Haskins took Mary to see a horseback riding exhibition in a field near town. At about 4:45 P.M. a sudden rainstorm brought the show to a premature end and scattered the audience. In recounting this episode, Mrs. Haskins's husband later reported that "it thundred and lightninged at such a degree as not remembered by the oldest person then in the town, also accompanied with heavy rain." Many people in the crowd took shelter in the nearby linhays—sheds with at least one open side. Mrs. Haskins, holding young Mary, sought shelter beneath a large elm tree. Two fifteen-year-old girls joined the nursemaid and child in this dangerous location.

"Mary had been a dull child before, but after this accident became lively and intelligent, and grew up so."

Suddenly there was a brilliant flash of lightning accompanied by "the most awful clap of thunder that any present ever remembered to have heard," reported the town's schoolmaster and historian, George Roberts. "All appeared deafened by the crash; after a momentary pause, a man gave the alarm, by pointing to a group that lay motionless under a tree. Some persons instantly ran to the spot, where there appeared three women and a child lying on the ground."

Mrs. Haskins and the two fifteen-year-old girls standing beneath the tree had been killed instantly by the lightning bolt. Young Mary Anning had been burned by the lightning and appeared to have stopped breathing. Only after the fifteen-month-old child was carried home to her parents did she open her eyes. According to an Anning family legend, "Mary had been a dull child before, but after this accident became lively and intelligent, and grew up so." Actually, being struck by lightning can't increase a person's intelligence, but similar storms did help Mary Anning make some important discoveries in the years ahead.

Mary's father built cabinets and other furniture in his carpentry shop located near the town jail. Although the family was far from wealthy, they managed to get by—until the night another tremendous storm struck, flooding the first floor of their home. It was said that Mary, Joseph, and their parents had to climb out an upstairs window to save their lives. Since he was a carpenter, Mr. Anning was able to rebuild his family's home, but the repairs were expensive. He needed to find a way to make more money.

By the early 1800s, scientists and collectors were becoming interested in fossils—the remains of ancient plants and animals. The cliffs and beaches in the Lyme Regis area were rich in fossils. In fact, the same kind of storms that nearly claimed Mary Anning's life and wrecked her family's house often ripped away chunks of the sea cliffs, exposing fossils that had been hidden for millions of years. On days when he wasn't working in his carpentry shop, Mr. Anning began collecting fossils along the seashore.

Mary Anning liked to draw;
she created this picture of a dog on a letter.

Sometimes he took Mary and Joseph along. Together they discovered fossil fish, and also spiral-shaped shells of ancient sea creatures called ammonites. It was said around Lyme Regis that Mary was so eager to find fossils that she never passed an unusual object on the ground without examining it to see if it was an ancient relic.

In addition to being a treasure trove for fossil hunters, Lyme Regis was a popular vacation resort. Each summer, visitors from London and other cities arrived to breathe the sea air and splash in the ocean. Like today's tourists, the summer visitors liked to bring home tokens of their vacation. All year Mary, Joseph, and their father would collect fossils, or *curiosities*, as many people called them in the early nineteenth century. In the summertime, the Annings would place their curiosities on a table outside Mr. Anning's carpentry shop, and Mary and Joseph would sell them to passing tourists. Mary felt proud whenever she sold a curiosity that she, her brother, or their father had found, for the money was a great help to her family.

[The Annings] were so impoverished that sometimes they didn't have enough to eat.

But scrambling along the sea cliffs was dangerous. On at least two occasions Richard Anning was nearly killed—once when he was caught in a rock slide and another time when he tumbled down a cliff in 1807. He never recovered from this terrible fall, and tuberculosis further eroded his health. Richard Anning died on November 5, 1810, when Mary was eleven and a half years old.

Though Molly, Joseph, and Mary Anning grieved for their husband and father, they also had a practical problem. They were suddenly desperately poor. Mary had to withdraw from the church school she had attended, because there was no money to send her. Fourteen-year-old Joseph obtained a job covering chairs. Besides Joseph's meager salary, the family received a small amount of charity, but they were so impoverished that sometimes they didn't have enough to eat.

Following his father's death, Joseph was so busy working that he had little time to hunt for curiosities. Mary, though, continued to go down to the seashore with the pick that her father had made for her. At first she searched for curiosities just to recall the happy times she had spent with her father. Then one day Mary was walking home carrying a beautiful ammonite she had found when a woman stopped her. The woman offered to buy the two-hundred-million-year-old fossil for a half crown, a coin worth about half an American dollar. That might not sound like much, but it would be worth about ten dollars today. As she exchanged the ammonite for the silver coin, Mary Anning realized that she had a way to help support her family.

Mary regularly explored the cliffs and beaches to search for fossils after that. The young girl climbing along the cliffs with her basket over her arm and her pick in her hand became a familiar sight in Lyme Regis. Mary and her mother sold the curiosities from a table outside Mr. Anning's old carpentry shop. The Annings' fossil business steadily grew and helped the family get by.

On his occasional days off, Joseph Anning hunted for curiosities either alone or with his sister. Sometime in 1811 Joseph discovered a fossil skull that was so large that he asked two men to help him dig it out from the rock along the shore. People who observed Joseph carrying the four-foot-long skull believed it had belonged to some kind of prehistoric crocodile, which was what Mary also thought when she saw it.

Joseph took Mary to the spot where he had found the skull, but there was no sign of the rest of the skeleton. Although Joseph didn't have time to continue the search, Mary did. She explored the area on and off for many months without coming upon any further trace of the creature.

Mary knew it was possible that only the skull had been preserved in the rock and that the rest of the skeleton no longer existed. She hoped, though, that the creature's fossilized skeleton lay hidden inside the cliff. If that was

First published in 1825, this drawing shows a girl who may be Mary Anning searching for fossils.

the case, a storm might eventually tear away just the right amount of the cliff, exposing the fossilized bones that went with the remarkable skull.

One night around late 1812, Lyme Regis was battered by a storm. Mary Anning may have been the only person in town who was pleased about it. The roar of the waves and the crashes of thunder were music to her ears as she lay in bed, since she hoped that the storm would uncover the skeleton.

The next day, Mary hurried to the place where Joseph had found the fossilized skull. She could hardly believe her luck. The storm had ripped away a portion of the cliff in exactly the right spot. Partway up the cliff she saw it—a monstrous skeleton at long last exposed to the light of day. Mary used her pick to remove some of the surrounding rock, but the skeleton was too massive for the thirteen-year-old to excavate without help.

Partway up the cliff she saw it–a monstrous skeleton at long last exposed to the light of day.

Mary found some workmen who agreed to help her excavate. The men followed Mary to the cliff and were about to remove the skeleton with their shovels when Mary had an idea. To prevent the ancient bones from being damaged, she asked the men to dig out the whole block of rock that contained the skeleton. When they hoisted the huge block of rock, Mary saw that the skeleton was gigantic—about twenty feet in length.

The people of Lyme Regis were then treated to a startling sight. Mary led the workmen as they carried the slab of rock containing the skeleton to the Anning house on Bridge Street. Mary's mother must have been astonished when she answered a knock at the door and saw a skeleton that was four times as long as her daughter was tall! In fact, the skeleton was so huge that it may have had to remain out on the street because it would not fit through the doorway.

Mary Anning paid the men a few pence (pennies) for their assistance.

Then, again with help, she fetched the skull that Joseph had found. Like the final piece of a jigsaw puzzle, the skull fit perfectly on the skeleton.

Word spread that a fossil skeleton resembling a huge crocodile had been discovered by a girl who lived in Lyme Regis, England. Scientists came to the Anning home to view the ancient creature and were amazed by what they saw. The bones had not belonged to any crocodile. Thirteen-year-old Mary Anning, with the help of her brother and a timely storm, had found the first complete skeleton of a fishlike reptile that swam in the ancient seas a hundred million years ago, in the age of the dinosaurs. At first people referred to the creature as "Mary's monster," and by similar names. Later, scientists adopted the name *Ichthyosaurus*, meaning "Fish Lizard."

Thirteen-year-old Mary Anning . . . had found the first complete skeleton of a fishlike reptile that swam in the ancient seas a hundred million years ago.

The Annings knew that the skeleton could not remain in the street, or in their cellar, where some believe it was temporarily housed. A collector for a museum soon purchased the skeleton from Mary. He paid her twenty-three British pounds for it. This was equal to about one hundred American dollars at the time and would be equivalent to about two thousand dollars today. Mary's discovery helped lift her family out of poverty and was big news in the scientific world. Eventually Mary Anning's *Ichthyosaurus* found a home in the famous British Museum in London.

Mary Anning grew up to become one of the greatest fossil hunters who ever lived. She didn't hunt alone, though. She found a four-legged assistant, or rather *he* found her. One day around 1820, Mary was "fossilizing," as she called it, when a small black and white dog trotted up to her. That evening the dog followed her home, and Mary adopted him. She named him Tray, and he became so attached to her that a portrait of Mary includes the little dog. Tray decided that his job was to guard Mary's fossils. Whenever she found an ancient fossil bone, Tray would keep the seabirds and people away until his mistress had dug it out.

Mary Anning and her dog found many ammonites and fish fossils together. They also made several discoveries as important as the *Ichthyosaurus*. In late 1823, when Mary was twenty-four years old, she came upon a nearly complete skeleton of a giant sea serpent that paddled through the water two hundred million years ago. This ancient animal, which the French naturalist Georges Cuvier called "the most amazing creature that was ever discovered," was the first of its kind ever unearthed. The long-necked sea creature was named *Plesiosaurus*, meaning "Lizard-like." Five years later, toward the end of 1828, Mary discovered the remains of a giant winged reptile that soared through the skies 150 million years ago. This flying creature was named *Pterosaur*, meaning "Winged Lizard."

Many scientists visited Lyme Regis to view Mary Anning's fossils or to purchase them for museums. Thanks in large part to her work, scientists learned that life on Earth extended further back in time and was more

An Ichthyosaurus *skeleton discovered by Mary Anning.*

Mary Anning with her beloved dog, Tray.

varied than had been believed. Her discoveries helped give birth to the science of *paleontology*—the study of prehistoric life. Because of her importance to this new science, the German naturalist and explorer Ludwig Leichhardt nicknamed Mary "the Princess of Paleontology."

Mary Anning was one of the first people to earn a living collecting fossils. Although she never became wealthy, she made enough money to buy a large house on Broad Street in Lyme Regis. Joseph married and established a home of his own, but Mary and her mother lived in the back of the Broad Street house and turned the front into a shop called Anning's Fossil Depot. To attract customers, Mary Anning placed an *Ichthyosaurus* skull and some beautiful ammonites in her shop window. Inside, Anning's

Dating from 1842, this is the only known drawing of Mary Anning's fossil shop.

Fossil Depot had "hundreds of fossils piled about in the greatest disorder," reported Dr. Gideon Mantell, one of many paleontologists who purchased fossils from her.

The Princess of Paleontology resented some of the scientists who visited her. "They suck my brains!" she complained to a friend, meaning that they won fame by writing about her fossils without giving her credit for discovering them. Her favorite customers were the children of Lyme Regis, who came to Anning's Fossil Depot to listen to Miss Anning talk about the time when Pterosaurs flew through the skies and dinosaurs roamed the earth. A rare description of Mary Anning was provided by Nellie Waring, who visited the unusual shop as a child and later wrote about her memories:

[Scientists] won fame by writing about her fossils without giving her credit for discovering them.

Miss Anning "The Fossil Woman" lived in Broad Street. In a house with a small shop front . . . there lived this very timid, very patient, and very celebrated woman, the discoverer of Ichthyosaurus *and of other fossil remains. We, as children, had large dealings with Miss Anning, our pocket-money was freely spent on the little Ammonites which she washed and burnished till they shone like metal, and on stones which took our childish fancy. She would serve us with the sweetest temper, bearing with all our little fancies and never finding us too troublesome as we turned over her trays of curiosities, and concluded by spending a few pence only. She must have been poor enough, for her little shop was scantily furnished, and her own dress always of the very plainest. She was very thin and had a high forehead, and large eyes which seemed to me to have a kindly consideration for her little customers.*

Mary and her dog had some brushes with disaster as they searched for fossils. Tray was killed in 1833 when a large chunk of a cliff broke off and crushed him. Several times Mary herself narrowly escaped from falling cliffs and giant waves. But it was cancer that killed the famous fossil hunter in 1847, when she was only forty-seven years old.

Following Mary Anning's death, some scientists put up a plaque in her memory near the cliffs where she had hunted for fossils most of her life. Other reminders of Mary are the fossils she discovered, housed today in museums around the world. The children of Lyme Regis remembered Mary Anning in their own way, with a little rhyme that recalled how her most famous discovery came as a result of her curiosity. Decades following Mary Anning's death, this rhyme about her was still known around the town:

Miss Anning, as a child, ne'er passed
A pin upon the ground;
But pick'd it up, and so at last
An Ichthyosaurus found.

iii Charles Goodyear

"The Rubber Man"

How different would our lives be if there were no rubber tires for cars, trucks, and bicycles? No rubber raincoats, rubber bands, rubber balls, rubber toys, rubber erasers, or rubber surgical gloves for surgeons? Though rubber plays an important role in modern life, the industry that creates rubber is relatively young. Not until the 1800s did it begin to become the giant business that it is today. The person who did the most to found the industry, Charles Goodyear, sacrificed his money, his freedom, and almost everything else he had as he searched for a way to make rubber useful.

Most natural rubber comes from *Hevea brasiliensis*, commonly called the rubber tree, which grows in hot, wet climates. Archaeologists have uncovered evidence that the Maya Indians of Central America and Mexico used rubber a thousand years ago. By the time Christopher Columbus reached the New World more than five centuries ago, the Indians of Mexico and South and Central America were using rubber to make containers, boots, clothing, and balls. The Indians of Peru referred

Indians tapping trees for rubber.

to rubber as *caoutchouc* (pronounced something like *koo-chook*), meaning "weeping tree." The name came from the fact that the rubber oozing from the rubber trees reminded them of teardrops.

One of the first written descriptions of rubber was made in the early 1600s by the Spanish historian Antonio de Herrera y Tordesillas. Herrera's book, *The General History of the Vast Continent and Islands of America*, contains a description of a ball game played by the Aztec Indians of Mexico. In this game, teams tried to propel a rubber ball, which "did bound and fly" so quickly that it "looked as if it had been alive," into goals on opposite sides of the court. The players bet gold, feathers, and even their clothes on the outcome of the game, which combined features of our modern basketball and soccer.

Starting in the 1500s, Spanish soldiers in the New World used rubber to waterproof their clothing. Rubber shoes, cloaks, and even toys were sent from the Americas back to Europe. But for several centuries, caoutchouc, as it was still known, was considered little more than a novelty by Europeans.

Charles Marie de La Condamine, a French explorer who visited Peru in 1735, gathered samples of caoutchouc and wrote descriptions of the substance. His work helped inspire the idea that caoutchouc might have great value. Joseph Priestley, an English scientist who later became one of the discoverers of oxygen, experimented with caoutchouc and in 1770 wrote that it was "excellently adapted to the purpose of wiping from paper the marks of a black lead pencil." Because it could rub out or erase mistakes, the substance became known in English as *rubber*, sometimes called *India rubber*. Rubber is still used to make erasers.

The rubber business didn't get rolling in Europe and the United States until the early 1800s. In 1820, London businessman Thomas Hancock founded the world's first rubber factory in England. Hancock imported blocks of rubber from South America, which he used to make items such as gloves and boots. A lot of extra rubber scraps were left over in the process. Hancock invented a machine that turned the scraps back into solid masses of rubber. He then was able to fashion the recycled rubber into additional wearing apparel.

In 1823 Charles Macintosh, a native of Glasgow, Scotland, patented a process to make waterproof raincoats. Macintosh sandwiched a layer of rubber between two layers of fabric. "Waterproof Double Textures," he called his raincoats, but customers called them macintoshes after their inventor. To this day, some people refer to raincoats as macintoshes.

There was a problem with rubber, however– a *big* problem. It changed with the seasons.

The first rubber company in the United States was begun in Roxbury, Massachusetts (now part of Boston), in early 1833. Called the Roxbury India Rubber Factory, the firm made shoes, coats, caps, life preservers, and other rubber goods. Boston became the center of the U.S. rubber industry, as five new firms also opened for business there in 1835.

There was a problem with rubber, however—a *big* problem. It changed with the seasons. Clothing and other items made of rubber turned as stiff as armor during the cold winter months. The same items became sticky and soft in hot weather. Rubber developed another unpleasant trait during the hot summer months. It smelled terrible!

Customers who had purchased rubber goods returned them to the manufacturers when they turned iron-hard in the winter or taffy-soft in the summer. One summer the Roxbury India Rubber Factory's owners dug a huge pit on their property, in which they buried hundreds of pairs of shoes and other rubber goods that had begun to melt and stink from the heat. The items that went into the ground were worth about $20,000—equivalent to about $400,000 in today's money.

During the 1830s one rubber firm after another went out of business, particularly in the United States, where there were broiling summers and frigid winters. Hundreds of workers lost their jobs, company owners went from riches to rags, and many tons of rubber were given away or destroyed. Unless a method was found to keep the substance stable with the seasons, the rubber boom would be remembered as a brief fad.

A person who would devote much of his life to improving rubber was born in New Haven, Connecticut, on December 29, 1800. Charles Goodyear was the oldest of six children of Amasa and Cynthia Bateman Goodyear. Charles's father was a hardware dealer and an inventor. One of his best-known inventions was a large steel fork used by farmers to pick up hay and manure.

When Charles was only four, his family moved about twenty miles to Naugatuck, Connecticut. Charles was a serious boy, and when not in school, he assisted his father in his hardware business and with the family farm.

In a book he later wrote about rubber, Charles recalled first encountering the substance in his youth. Referring to himself in the third person, he explained: "When yet a schoolboy, the wonderful and mysterious properties of this substance attracted his attention. A thin scale [of rubber], peeled from a bottle or a shoe, attracted his attention, and suggested to him that it would be very useful, if it could be so prepared as to prevent its becoming [soft], as it soon did from the warmth and pressure of his hand."

On Charles's seventeenth birthday, his father signed him up for an apprenticeship at Rogers & Brothers, a large hardware firm in Philadelphia, Pennsylvania. The young apprentice learned the hardware business by working ten to twelve hours a day. Charles stood only a little over five feet in height and suffered from lifelong poor health, including chronic indigestion. Upon completing his apprenticeship at age twenty-one, Charles wanted to remain in Philadelphia and begin his own hardware business, but illness prevented it. He returned home to recuperate and then went back to work for his father. He also began to court Clarissa Beecher, an innkeeper's daughter whom he had known since they were children. Charles and Clarissa were married in August of 1824 and over the years would have nine children together—five daughters and four sons.

Charles Goodyear

For several years, Charles and his father made farm implements and operated a hardware business called A. Goodyear & Sons. In 1826 Charles moved to Philadelphia with his wife and their first child, Ellen. There, with his brother Robert's help, he opened a branch store of the family hardware business. The Philadelphia store flourished, and Charles began selling hoes, hay-and-manure forks, scythes (implements with blades used for mowing), and other goods to customers in other states. He also became a partner in two inventions created by other people—a cutting device and a self-winding clock. The Goodyear firm was doing so well that Charles and his relatives appeared to be on the road to wealth.

Disaster struck in 1829. About then, the U.S. economy ran into one of its periodic hard times. Customers who owed the Goodyears money couldn't pay their bills. In turn, the Goodyears couldn't repay loans they had taken out to establish their business and purchase goods to sell. To make things worse, the inventions in which Charles had invested sold poorly. Worry over money probably contributed to several weeks of illness during which Charles suffered from severe stomach cramps and fever.

Americans had more reason to worry about their debts in Charles Goodyear's time than they do today, for people who couldn't pay what they owed often landed in debtors' prisons. The Goodyears had to pledge to pay the money they owed to avoid being arrested and jailed. Charles had to move his hardware business into a smaller store to reduce his rent payments.

Piece by piece, the Goodyears were forced to liquidate their business, yet they still owed thousands. Charles felt largely to blame, for he had expanded the operation to other states and had invested in the failed inventions. Besides, his father was nearly sixty years old. Charles couldn't let him go to debtors' prison. So Charles Goodyear, now about thirty, assumed responsibility for the remaining $12,000 debt—equal to about

$240,000 today. Amasa and Cynthia lost their home and farm back in Connecticut and moved to Philadelphia to live with Charles and his family.

How would Charles make a living? Although his investment in the cutting device and the self-winding clock had not worked out, Charles had been infected by the inventing bug. Two giant obstacles stood in the way of his becoming an inventor: He had no scientific background and little talent for building things. If he attempted to become an inventor it would bring utter ruin on Goodyear and his loved ones, predicted his friends and relatives. Nonetheless, he became convinced of the seemingly ridiculous idea that he was destined to create a great invention.

Two giant obstacles stood in the way of his becoming an inventor: He had no scientific background and little talent for building things.

For many years it appeared that the doomsayers would be proven right about Charles Goodyear. Although he did create several inventions, none made much money. In 1831 he patented something called a "safe-eye button." The next year he concocted a new method for making spoons as well as a new kind of faucet. But to support his family, he had to borrow more and more money, which landed him deeper and deeper into debt.

Charles's obsession with rubber began in 1834. That summer, while in New York City, he entered a shop that sold rubber goods. The store was a branch of the Roxbury India Rubber Factory—the firm that had lost a fortune burying spoiled shoes and other rubber items. While in the store, Charles picked up a rubber life preserver and carefully scrutinized it. The valve through which the preserver was inflated with air had been poorly designed, he decided. Certain that he could invent a better valve, he purchased the life preserver and took it back to Philadelphia with him.

Several months later, he returned to the store with an improved valve of his own design. But when he offered to sell it to the company, he met with disappointment. Rubber was a dying industry, and the company wouldn't be interested in his improved valve, the store manager confided. But if someone could find a way to prevent rubber from turning hard like iron in the winter and sticky and soft in the summer, *that* would be a discovery for the ages. Besides becoming rich and famous, the inventor would help introduce many useful items to the world.

Ellen later recalled that her father sometimes "took possession of our kitchen for a work-shop."

Charles Goodyear took some raw rubber back home with him—along with the conviction that *he* was the person who would rescue the rubber industry. Over the next few years, he moved about a great deal with Clarissa and the children, often to be near places where he could obtain rubber and find facilities where he could conduct experiments. Besides Philadelphia, Charles and his family lived in such places as New Haven and Naugatuck, Connecticut; New York City; and Boston, Lynn, and Woburn, Massachusetts.

Charles Goodyear's daughter Ellen later recalled that her father sometimes "took possession of our kitchen for a work-shop." He tried many methods to make rubber more stable. He treated rubber with acids, developed what was known as the acid-gas process, and mixed it with powdered magnesia, lead, quicklime, and other ingredients. He purchased a variety of chemicals from pharmacists and used them to treat rubber, but nothing worked very well.

While in New Haven, Charles, along with family members and several other helpers, stitched together hundreds of pairs of shoes in his home workshop. Charles expected to turn a handsome profit from the shoes, but unfortunately they turned soft in the heat and did not make the family any money.

In about 1838, Goodyear met fellow rubber scientist Nathaniel Hayward, who had discovered that sulfur could help make rubber more durable. Goodyear bought the rights to the process from Hayward. Combining some of his own methods with Hayward's sulfur process, Goodyear made shoes and other items that were more durable than earlier rubber goods. The U.S. Postal Service was so impressed that it ordered 150 rubber mailbags from Goodyear. Committed to delivering mail in all kinds of weather, the postal service hoped rubber mailbags would do a good job of keeping out moisture.

At last, success seemed to be just around the corner, for if the mailbags worked there would probably be a flood of government orders for rubber goods. Charles Goodyear made 150 rubber mailbags in a factory in Woburn, Massachusetts. He felt so confident about the sturdy-looking bags that he hung them from hooks in the Woburn factory and invited people to come see them. He then went out of town for two weeks. Upon his return, he was crushed to find that the mailbags were a sticky mess. Due to heat, the rubber had softened, and the bags had either broken off from their handles or were sagging. Of course, the post office would not pay for the gooey bags.

Charles continued his experiments, writing down ideas in a journal that he kept by his bed at night. To test the results of his latest experiments—and to advertise rubber—he began wearing clothing that he had made out of the substance. Reportedly a man who asked how he might recognize Charles Goodyear was told: "If you meet a man who has on an India rubber cap, [scarf], coat, vest, and shoes, with an India rubber money purse without a cent of money in it, that is he."

Goodyear was so obsessed with rubber that people called him the "India Rubber Man," and sometimes the "India Rubber Maniac." According to his friend John Haskins, "Many thought him almost insane" because of all that he had sacrificed for his rubber experiments.

For example, he repeatedly sacrificed his freedom. While experimenting with rubber, Charles sank even deeper into debt. Now and then people to whom he owed money had him locked in debtors' prison. Among the places where Charles Goodyear spent time in prison were Philadelphia, Boston, New York City, and his birthplace of New Haven, Connecticut. It was said that while serving time in a Philadelphia debtors' prison, Goodyear was allowed to work on his rubber experiments.

Goodyear may have suffered from lead poisoning as a result of all of his experiments involving rubber and lead.

His health also suffered. One day in about 1835, Goodyear was treating rubber with gas vapors in a closed room when he began feeling woozy and fainted. He was discovered unconscious, pulled from the room, and revived. Charles developed a fever, however, and had to remain under a doctor's care for six weeks. His digestive problems caused him misery, especially in times of stress. He also suffered from painful joint aches, which doctors diagnosed as gout. Today it is believed that Goodyear may have suffered from lead poisoning as a result of all of his experiments involving rubber and lead. His joint pain grew so bad that at times he could only walk with the aid of a cane or crutches.

Charles Goodyear is often portrayed as heroic for sacrificing so much for the sake of his dream. But he made one sacrifice that is difficult to excuse. While he experimented with rubber, his wife and children sometimes had to do without the essentials of life. His family's only food often consisted of half-grown potatoes dug from their garden, and bullfrogs and turtles caught in nearby streams. Charles also frequented pawnbrokers' shops, where he sold many of the family's possessions for a little cash. At one point things became so bad that he auctioned his children's schoolbooks for five dollars.

Of Clarissa and Charles's nine children, two daughters and two sons died very young. It wasn't unusual for about a third of all children to die of disease before age fifteen in the mid-1800s, so the Goodyear family wasn't far from typical. But in this case poor nutrition and inadequate protection from the winter cold may have contributed to the children's deaths.

The answer that the India Rubber Man gave up so much to find and that had eluded him for nearly five years came suddenly and unexpectedly. There are numerous versions of what happened, so the precise details will probably never be known. But the basic facts can be ascertained from Charles Goodyear's book *Gum-Elastic and Its Varieties.*

In early 1839 Goodyear entered a building in Woburn, Massachusetts, that contained a hot stove. The place may have been the factory where he had made the mailbags, or perhaps it was a house or store in town. Goodyear often carried a piece of rubber with him, which he liked to hold in his hands the way a sculptor might absentmindedly hold a piece of clay. On this particular day, he was holding a piece of rubber combined with sulfur as he stood near a hot stove, talking to his brother Nelson Goodyear and several other men. Suddenly the rubber slipped from his hands, so that, in his own words, it was "brought in contact with the hot stove." But instead of softening and becoming sticky, the rubber seemed to become tougher as a result of the intense heat.

Charles Goodyear was astonished. It was common knowledge that at rather high temperatures rubber lost its shape and became mushy. In fact, manufacturers warned customers not to place rubber in contact with temperatures of 100 degrees Fahrenheit or higher. Likewise, rubber experimenters had always viewed heat as an enemy and had tried to avoid it. But apparently at much higher temperatures—roughly 300 degrees Fahrenheit—rubber that was mixed with sulfur became stronger.

CHARLES GOODYEAR
Safety Pioneer
WHO DISCOVERED VULCANIZED RUBBER 100 YEARS AGO
1839 · 1939

Artist's version of the discovery of vulcanization.

Goodyear was extremely excited by his accidental discovery, but he had many questions. Was this a one-time fluke that had occurred for unknown reasons, or was intense heat truly the answer? Did the process make a permanent change in the rubber, or was it just temporary? What temperature worked best, and how long should the rubber be cooked? According to Goodyear's account, following the accident at the stove he began experimenting with the new process, often in his family's home in Woburn.

"Upon further trial with heat," Goodyear wrote, "[I] was further convinced by finding that India rubber could not be melted in boiling sulfur at any heat ever so great, but always charred."

Ellen Goodyear, who was about fourteen years old at the time, sometimes helped her father as he worked with rubber. Later Ellen recalled how thrilled her father was to discover that his new process protected rubber from cold as well as heat:

> *As I was passing in and out of the room, I casually observed the little piece of [rubber], which he was holding near the fire. He nailed the piece of [rubber] outside the kitchen door in the intense cold. In the morning he brought it in, holding it up exultingly. He had found it perfectly flexible, as it was when he put it out. This was proof enough of the value of the discovery.*

By careful experimentation Goodyear answered all of his questions. The change was real and permanent. He also learned many important points, such as that the sulfur had to be bone dry and free of acid, and that his heaters and fires had to be operated so as to raise the heat gradually and evenly to about 270 degrees Fahrenheit. Charles Goodyear's process of toughening rubber through the use of chemicals and intense heat was named *vulcanization*, for Vulcan, the ancient Roman god of fire.

Vulcanization took several years to catch on. There had been so many false hopes regarding rubber in the past that people were slow to place faith in the new process. Besides, Charles Goodyear had spent so much time experimenting, and was so deeply in debt, that he wasn't able to promote vulcanization effectively at first. In fact, some of the roughest times for Goodyear and his family came *after* he discovered vulcanization.

In early 1840, Goodyear was again arrested for debt. After Clarissa and his father got him released, Charles took to his bed with a fever. It was wintertime, and having run out of items to pawn, his family had no food to eat or fuel to keep them warm. Still weak, Goodyear rose from his sickbed and walked several miles through a driving snowstorm to the home of Oliver Coolidge, a Woburn man who had shown him kindness. On the way, he had to rest frequently on snowbanks. The inventor reached the Coolidge house in terrible condition, but he obtained a loan that helped his family survive the winter.

In 1844 Charles Goodyear received a patent from the U.S. government for his vulcanization process. Rubber companies began to pay him royalties for the right to use his method. By 1850 the rubber business was on its way toward becoming the giant industry it is today. Although not wealthy, the Goodyears were finally lifted out of poverty.

Charles Goodyear was always insulted when people asserted that the solution to the rubber problem had just fallen into his lap. In 1853 he published *Gum-Elastic and Its Varieties*. An unusual aspect of this book is that at least one copy was printed on rubber rather than on paper! While admitting that luck had played an important role in his discovery, Goodyear insisted in his book that he had been prepared to take advantage of it:

> *I was for many years seeking to accomplish this object and allowed nothing to escape my notice that related to it. Like the fall-*

ing apple before Newton's gaze, it [the accident with the rubber and the stove] was suggestive of an important fact to one whose mind was previously prepared to draw an inference from any occurrence which might favor the object of his research. While I admit that these discoveries of mine were not the result of scientific chemical investigation, I am not willing to admit that they were the result of what is commonly called accident. I claim them to be the result of the closest application and observation.

Goodyear lived to discover about five hundred uses for rubber, and to see about sixty thousand people employed in the growing rubber industry.

Although Charles Goodyear never designed rubber tires, his work was a great boost to the tire industry; this photograph shows the inside of an early tire factory.

In his era, all rubber was natural, meaning that it came from rubber trees and other plants. Later, scientists learned how to make synthetic rubber out of chemicals. Today, natural and synthetic rubbers are used to produce fifty thousand different items, and the vulcanization process is still a vital part of rubber manufacturing. Much of the rubber supply in the United States goes into the making of tires. Although Charles Goodyear never designed rubber tires, the Goodyear Tire & Rubber Company was named in his honor. The inventor, who according to U.S. Patents Commissioner Joseph Holt had shown "almost superhuman perseverance" in his work, died in 1860 at the age of fifty-nine.

Anesthesia iv

"The Greatest Discovery Ever Made"

Scene I: Early one morning in the year 1840, a patient knocks on the door of a doctor's home. Judging by his expression, you might think the patient is about to be tortured, which is close to the truth, for he is about to endure an operation. The man is led to the "operating room"—really just a room of the doctor's house—where he is given whiskey to drink. After two glassfuls, the patient relaxes a bit, but when the doctor tells him to lie on the operating table he is gripped by such fear that he tries to run away. Two strong assistants waiting nearby catch the patient and strap him to the table. With mounting terror the patient watches the doctor remove his saw and other instruments from a drawer. "No!" he cries, yanking at the straps with all his might. During the next few minutes the patient experiences indescribable pain as the doctor cuts through his skin and probes with his instruments.

Scene II: The time is the present, the place a modern hospital operating room. A patient is being prepared for cancer surgery. Although the patient expected to be terrified, as the operation approaches she finds that she is eager to get rid of her tumor. The anesthesiologist injects medication into the intravenous catheter, or tube, that has been placed in her arm and assures her that she will be fine. Once the patient is asleep, the operation begins. She remains unconscious throughout the procedure, oblivious of the fact that the surgeon is removing her tumor. Following the operation, she is wheeled to the recovery room, where she receives more medication through her catheter to control her postoperative pain. The operation was a success, the surgeon informs her the next day. She has had minimal pain, she tells her anesthesiologist, and recalls nothing about the operation.

Many people chose to die rather than undergo the pain of surgery, and many others chose to walk around with a mouthful of rotting teeth.

Anesthetics are what doctors and dentists give people to put them to sleep or dull pain during operations and other medical and dental procedures. Few people go through life without being anesthetized several times. Dental patients are routinely given anesthetics before having teeth pulled. Anesthetics are administered to patients who need to have their tonsils or appendix removed. Every day, thousands of patients around the world undergo operations—ranging from the removal of a wart to heart surgery—while under the influence of anesthetics. Women often receive anesthetics before childbirth.

Anesthesia is a surprisingly recent discovery, dating from the 1840s. Before then, doctors couldn't perform operations that are routine today because the pain would kill the patient. In fact, many people chose to die rather than undergo the pain of surgery, and many others chose to walk around with a mouthful of rotting teeth rather than face the torture of dental work.

By the early 1840s, there was only one known "anesthetic" for cases in

This woodcut from a book published in 1517 is one of the oldest pictures of a surgical amputation.

which surgery was attempted. Whiskey was poured down patients' throats to make them drunk. It was said that many a surgeon entered an operating room carrying *two* bottles of whiskey—one for the patient and the other for himself, so that he could withstand the patient's shrieks. Whiskey wasn't an effective anesthetic, though, so the patient generally had to be strapped down to the table and held still by the surgeon's burly assistants.

In 1779 the English chemist Humphry Davy breathed nitrous oxide, which made him act so silly that he nicknamed it "laughing gas."

The development of anesthetics revolutionized medicine, yet the story is not well known. The main reason is that historians disagree on who should be credited with the discovery: Georgia physician Crawford Long, Connecticut dentists Horace Wells and William Morton, or Boston chemist Charles Jackson. All four men sought credit for the discovery and became involved in a battle that resulted in tragic consequences for all but one of them.

The substances that became the first true anesthetics—ether and nitrous oxide—were known long before they were put to medical use. The Swiss doctor Theophrastus Bombastus von Hohenheim, who was known as Paracelsus, experimented with ether by the early 1540s. Paracelsus exposed animals to ether and wrote: "It is taken even by chickens, and they fall asleep from it for a while but awaken later without harm." Ether "quiets all suffering, and relieves all pain," he added. Nitrous oxide was discovered by the English scientist Joseph Priestley in 1772. In 1779 the English chemist Humphry Davy breathed nitrous oxide, which made him act so silly that he nicknamed it "laughing gas." Nitrous oxide could "probably be used with advantage during surgical operations," Davy concluded. However, no one used laughing gas or ether as a surgical anesthetic for many more years.

There is a popular belief that drug abuse is a recent phenomenon. In truth, people have abused alcohol and other substances for thousands of years. By 1840, two of the most commonly abused substances in the United States were ether and laughing gas. At gatherings called "ether frolics" and "laughing-gas parties," people sniffed these substances, sometimes dying in the process. In addition, "nitrous oxide demonstrations" were a popular form of entertainment.

Self-styled "professors" packed containers of laughing gas onto horse-drawn carts, then traveled about, giving demonstrations at meeting halls and tent shows. Typically it cost a quarter to attend one of these demonstrations. Once the audience was seated, the "professor" would stride out onto the stage. Science, he would explain, had found a substance that could magically transform people who inhaled it. Several of his assistants would breathe the gas from silk bags and start laughing and dancing around the stage. After they calmed down, the "professor" would present a lecture about nitrous oxide—to remind everyone that they had come for "educational reasons." Finally the moment arrived that everyone was awaiting: the professor asked for volunteers to come breathe the gas.

Soon the audience was roaring with amusement as respected community members breathed the gas and began giggling, performing somersaults, and dancing across the stage. The "professor" might end his visit to town by selling some of his nitrous oxide supply for private "laughing-gas parties."

Jefferson, Georgia, was among the numerous American towns where "laughing-gas parties" were held. In that town of five hundred people there lived a young doctor named Crawford Long, who had been born in nearby Danielsville, Georgia, on the day after Halloween of 1815.

On evenings when he had no medical emergencies, Dr. Long and his friends would meet in his office to talk and play chess, checkers, and the card game known as whist. At one such session, his friends asked Long to provide them with laughing gas. He had no apparatus for preparing nitrous oxide, the young physician said, but he would supply them with ether instead. It should be pointed out that although the United States had no drug abuse laws yet, it was wrong for a physician to hand out a dangerous substance like ether for nonmedical reasons. But Dr. Long supplied the ether and took part in the "ether frolics" that began in December of 1841.

As he and his friends stumbled about after inhaling ether, Dr. Long observed that they sometimes smashed into furniture or fell without seeming to suffer pain. "Didn't you feel that?" he would ask his friends. "They assured me that they did not feel the least pain from these accidents,"

Dr. Crawford Long

Dr. Long later recalled. Actually, it was common for people cavorting around under the influence of ether or laughing gas to suffer accidents—sometimes causing profuse bleeding—without seeming to care. But until Dr. Crawford Long, no one had thought much about it.

The participants in the "ether frolics" in Jefferson included James Venable. A student in his early twenties, Venable had repeatedly asked his friend Dr. Long to remove two small tumors from the back of his neck. Each time Dr. Long set a date for cutting away the tumors, however, Venable thought of the pain he would be subjected to and backed out.

One day as Dr. Long watched his friends bump into things under the influence of ether, an idea popped into his head. On March 30, 1842, he said to Venable: "We have received bruises while under the influence of ether without suffering, so probably an operation could be performed under its influence without pain." Young Venable agreed to have one of the growths removed that evening.

This time Venable kept the appointment. Dr. Long sat him in a chair, then poured ether on a towel, which he placed near Venable's nose. The patient soon fell asleep. Instead of the usual screams of pain that accompanied surgery, Venable slept peacefully through the operation. When it was over and Venable awoke, he was at first disappointed, for he thought the procedure hadn't yet begun. Not until Dr. Long showed him the half-inch growth he had removed did Venable realize the truth. In his record book, Dr. Long wrote: "James Venable, March 30, 1842, Ether and Exsecting Tumor, $2.00."

This was the first operation in history in which a true anesthetic was used. Dr. Crawford Long would have become a medical hero, hundreds of schools and hospitals would have been named for him, and November 1 (his birthday) might have become a holiday—if not for one thing. The first definition of *discover* in the dictionary is "to make known." To go down in history as a discovery, a breakthrough must be revealed to the world so that all of humanity can benefit.

Dr. Long should have written an article describing his serendipitous insight about anesthesia and his operation on James Venable. Instead he kept his breakthrough to himself for several years. When I visited the Crawford Long Museum in Jefferson, Georgia, the staff explained that, as a country doctor, Dr. Long was so busy delivering babies and treating patients that he had no time to write an article for a medical journal. It was true that as his practice grew he had little time for chess, whist, or writing, and that he was even late for his own wedding because he had to stay with a sick patient. Dr. Long himself later offered another reason for not picking up his pen. As a young, small-town physician, he explained, he lacked the confidence to claim that he had made a major discovery. Another factor was that like a lot of people, Crawford Long had trouble sitting down to write. The bottom line was that his silence deprived the world of the benefits of anesthesia.

Dr. Wells was a shy and sensitive man who was deeply disturbed by the fact that his dental work inflicted pain on his patients.

Over the next few years Dr. Long performed several more operations using ether, and he administered ether to a number of women, including his own wife, in childbirth. But knowledge of his ether work didn't travel much beyond Jefferson, Georgia, until he published an article in the *Southern Medical and Surgical Journal* in December of 1849. By then thousands of patients had continued to suffer pain during surgery and three other men had claimed the discovery of anesthesia.

The story continues a thousand miles to the north of Georgia in Hartford, Connecticut. At the time that Crawford Long was operating on James Venable, Horace Wells was practicing dentistry in Hartford. Born in Vermont on January 21, 1815, Dr. Wells was a shy and sensitive man who was deeply disturbed by the fact that his dental work inflicted pain on his patients. He was also very inventive, creating such contraptions as a shower in which the water was pumped by foot. Despite his inventiveness he was frustrated at being unable to find a way to make dental work less painful.

On the evening of December 10, 1844, Dr. Horace Wells and his wife attended a nitrous oxide demonstration at Hartford's Union Hall. "Professor" Gardner Colton gave a talk on nitrous oxide and demonstrated its effects on his assistants. The audience hooted as the men stumbled and pranced about on the stage. When Colton asked the audience for volunteers, Horace Wells shocked his wife by going forward. The usually shy dentist was determined to experience the effects of the gas for himself.

Dr. Horace Wells

Dr. Wells inhaled the gas with the other volunteers onstage. Soon they were jumping and dancing about, but Dr. Wells could think clearly enough to notice something. Under the influence of the laughing gas, a young drugstore clerk named Samuel Cooley hit his legs on a bench very hard. Although blood oozed through his trousers, Cooley did not seem to notice the injury. Samuel Cooley's accidental injury would prove to be a stroke of luck for humanity.

After the volunteers returned to their seats, Wells pointed to the blood seeping through Cooley's trousers and commented, "You must have hurt yourself."

"No," responded Cooley, surprised to see the blood. Wells kept his eyes on Cooley and could tell that he felt no pain from his injury until the effects of the laughing gas wore off.

At the end of the show, Dr. Wells approached "Professor" Colton and asked, "Why cannot a man have a tooth extracted under the gas and not feel it?" Colton thought it was possible and agreed to bring a bag of laughing gas to Wells's office the next day.

Wells, who was himself suffering from a troublesome wisdom tooth, arranged for fellow dentist John Riggs to come to his office the next morning. Colton delivered the nitrous oxide, and Wells sat in his own dental chair and breathed it through a tube until he fell asleep. While Wells was unconscious, Dr. Riggs gripped his wisdom tooth with a dental forceps, wiggled it, then pulled it from the bone. Wells awoke to see Dr. Riggs holding his tooth.

"I felt it no more than the prick of a pin!" Wells said excitedly. "It is the greatest discovery ever made!"

During the next several weeks, Wells and Riggs gave laughing gas to approximately a dozen patients and then performed dental surgery on them. The high-strung Wells was so excited by the success of laughing gas as an anesthetic that he could hardly eat or sleep. All night he would lie awake, pondering the best way to present his discovery to the medical world.

If he could perform a successful demonstration in the metropolis of Boston, Massachusetts, he decided, the news would quickly spread around the world. Wells went to Boston and arranged to do a demonstration with the nation's leading surgeon, Dr. John Collins Warren, who had founded Massachusetts General Hospital in that city. The demonstration took place in a hall near the hospital around January 21, 1845—the date of Wells's thirtieth birthday. Dr. Warren had already witnessed a number of unsuccessful attempts to anesthetize patients, including the use of hypnotism, so he had absolutely no faith in Wells. "There is a gentleman here," Dr. Warren told the doctors and medical students in the hall, "who pretends he has something which will destroy pain in surgical operations." Expecting failure, the audience snickered at Horace Wells, who was trembling with nervousness.

"I felt it no more than the prick of a pin! It is the greatest discovery ever made!"

Wells hadn't brought a patient because he knew that in any large group several people were bound to need dental work. Was anyone in the audience willing to have a tooth extracted under the influence of laughing gas? A young man came forward and sat in a chair. Dr. Wells put the patient to sleep with laughing gas, then pulled the diseased tooth. At this point luck again enters the story, only this time it was very *bad* luck. When Dr. Wells pulled his tooth, the patient groaned. Already in a skeptical mood from Dr. Warren's sarcastic introduction, the audience hissed and shouted "Swindler!" and "Humbug!" Horace Wells, who later blamed himself for "removing the gas bag too soon," fled the lecture hall amid the laughter.

Actually, had anyone bothered to ask the patient, the audience would have learned that the demonstration was a success. The patient later explained that he had "felt practically no pain" during the tooth extraction. But Dr. Warren had put the audience in the mood to anticipate failure, and because of one groan, no one questioned the patient. Ironically, following Wells's demonstration, the medical students went off to entertain themselves by—of all things—inhaling laughing gas!

Had Dr. Warren and the audience been open-minded, Horace Wells would have been hailed as the discoverer of anesthesia. But Wells must shoulder some of the blame himself, for he gave up too easily. Back in Hartford, he continued to administer laughing gas successfully to dozens of dental patients. Had he published an article in 1845 or convinced the Boston doctors to come and see him work in Hartford, he still might have received the recognition he deserved. But, like Crawford Long down in Georgia, Horace Wells remained silent. He was too humiliated over what he considered his "failure" to fight for his cause. By the spring of 1845 he was suffering from a mental breakdown and had to temporarily retire from dentistry. This cleared the way for two other men to stake their claims to the discovery of anesthesia.

William Morton was born on August 9, 1819, in a small farmhouse in Charlton, Massachusetts, forty-five miles southwest of Boston. In those days families with a roof over their heads and crops to eat didn't consider themselves poor, but William grew up in what were called modest circumstances. As a youth, he was threatened with expulsion from school for something he didn't do. To remain in school, he was simply required to apologize to the teacher. But William, who was as high-strung as Horace Wells but also proud and stubborn, refused. He was thrown out of school and grew up to be a moody young man, always willing to fight for himself to get ahead.

Morton dreamed of becoming a physician but, lacking money for medical school, settled on dentistry. In those days the main way of becoming a dentist was by studying under an established dentist. By 1841 Morton was studying with Dr. Horace Wells in Hartford, Connecticut. The next year, at the age of twenty-three, Dr. Morton set up his own practice in Farmington, Connecticut, just ten miles from Wells's office in Hartford.

Morton and Horace Wells became close friends. When Wells created a gold solder that held artificial teeth in place, he and Morton formed a partnership and moved to Boston to try and make their fortune with the invention. The solder did not catch on as well as the two young dentists had hoped, however, and Horace Wells was too homesick to give it much of a chance. He soon pulled out of the partnership and returned to Hartford, but William Morton saw Boston as the place where he would become rich

Dr. William Morton

and famous. He remained there and built up a large dental practice.

When Horace Wells gave his infamous demonstration in Boston in early 1845, he brought along his friend William Morton to assist him. Although Wells was laughed out of the hall, his use of laughing gas inspired Morton to think about anesthesia. Something else put Morton on the trail. In Boston he lived for a time at the home of Dr. Charles Jackson, an eminent physician, dentist, chemist, and geologist. During tooth extractions, Jackson told Morton, he gave patients "toothache drops" composed of ether. He didn't have them breathe the drops but just applied them to their gums to reduce pain. Morton began applying Jackson's toothache drops onto teeth to numb them prior to dental work. He also began considering how ether could be used more effectively.

Although Wells was laughed out of the hall, his use of laughing gas inspired Morton to think about anesthesia.

Morton established an estate outside Boston which became known as Etherton because of the experiments he performed there. First he experimented on animals, including his family's water spaniel, who kept him company in his laboratory. One day the dog breathed too much ether and nearly died. Another time, as Morton was trying to etherize the dog, the animal knocked over the jar of ether. This was another serendipitous accident with important consequences, for Morton saved the remaining ether and decided to use it to experiment on himself. He poured ether onto his handkerchief, sat down, and inhaled it until he drifted off to sleep.

Wanting to make further experiments, he obtained a new supply of ether and tested it on two former assistants. But instead of falling asleep, both young men began shouting and leaping about. Morton was confused. Why did the first batch of ether put the dog and himself to sleep while the second batch had a different effect on his two assistants?

Morton went to question Dr. Charles Jackson about ether but didn't want him to know why, because Jackson had a reputation for trying to steal other people's discoveries. Jackson was born into a wealthy and prominent family in Plymouth, Massachusetts, on June 21, 1805. The mansion that was his childhood home is now the headquarters for the Mayflower Society, an organization dedicated to the memory of the Pilgrims who founded Plymouth in 1620. Jackson attended Harvard Medical School, won prizes, and wrote hundreds of scientific articles on many subjects. Although regarded as a genius, Jackson was not happy; while he was good at many things, he yearned to make some great discovery.

Jackson *claimed* to be the brains behind a discovery on several occasions. For example, he insisted that he gave Samuel Morse the idea for the

Dr. Charles Jackson

telegraph during an ocean voyage in the fall of 1832. Although Jackson's advice may have helped, no one took his claim seriously, and Samuel Morse is remembered as the inventor of the telegraph.

So, without explaining why, Dr. William Morton asked Jackson questions about ether. Jackson showed him some ether in his laboratory. While Morton studied the sweet-smelling liquid, Jackson said, "This ether has been standing for some time." Ether had to be highly refined and fresh to work properly, he told Morton.

Thrilled that he at last knew the secret, Morton began dancing about, yelling "Eureka! Eureka!"

Suddenly the young dentist understood. His first batch of ether had been of good quality, but his second batch, which he had obtained from another source, had been impure.

Morton headed to the chemical firm where he had bought his first batch and purchased a new flask of the colorless liquid. He carried it to his dental office in Boston, sat in his dental chair, and breathed the ether until he fell asleep. When he awoke and checked the time, he was amazed to discover that he had been unconscious for about eight minutes, for to him it had seemed that only an instant had elapsed. Morton attempted to stand, but he felt so groggy that he fell back into the dental chair. Slowly his brain cleared, and he regained control over his limbs. Thrilled that he at last knew the secret—that ether had to be highly refined and fresh in order to be useful to doctors and dentists—Morton began dancing about, yelling "Eureka! Eureka!"

Over the next few days he performed several painless dental procedures on patients using ether. In early October of 1846 he visited Dr. John Collins Warren, whose hostile attitude had devastated Dr. Horace Wells more than a year and a half earlier. Warren promised to inform Morton of the first opportunity for anesthetizing a surgical patient.

Morton's chance came on the morning of Friday, October 16, 1846. In an operating theater now known as the Ether Dome at Massachusetts General Hospital, Morton put a patient to sleep with ether. As approximately one hundred doctors, students, and others looked on, Dr. Warren cut away a growth from beneath the jaw of the patient, who slept through the operation without stirring. After the surgery was over, Morton asked the awakening patient: "Did you feel any pain?"

"No," he replied.

Realizing that he had just taken part in an event that would transform medicine, Dr. John Collins Warren told the audience: "Gentlemen, *this* is no humbug."

News of the discovery spread around the world. A New York City newspaper called Morton's breakthrough "the most glorious discovery of

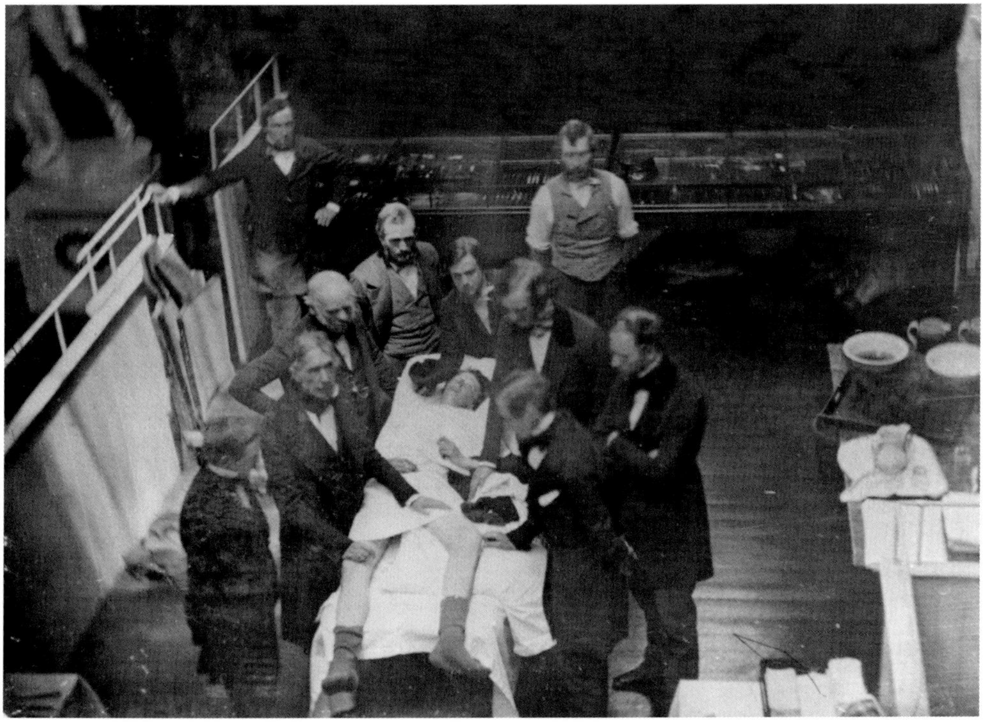

Dating from 1847, this is one of the earliest photographs of an operation with an anesthetic; the patient is undergoing surgery in the Ether Dome at Massachusetts General Hospital.

this or any other age." The *People's Journal* of London, England, declared: "Hail, happy hour! WE HAVE CONQUERED PAIN." In Russia, they called it "the greatest blessing, a gift from heaven." Dr. Oliver Wendell Holmes, a famous Boston doctor and writer, coined the name *anesthesia*, meaning "without feeling."

Ether, laughing gas, and other anesthetics gradually came into general use, helping to prevent pain and save many thousands of lives. But the question remained: Who actually discovered anesthesia?

At first most people credited William Morton. But then Wells wrote an article recounting how he had observed people endure "severe blows" after inhaling laughing gas, which had led to the dental procedure in early 1845 in which the patient had unfortunately groaned. At the time, Dr. Warren and the onlookers hadn't been ready to give anesthesia a fair chance, yet the fact was that the patient hadn't felt much pain.

Feeling that he was being cheated out of the credit due him, Dr. Charles Jackson asserted that *he* was the real discoverer. Hadn't his "toothache drops" given Morton the idea for anesthesia? Hadn't he told Morton the crucial information that the ether had to be highly refined and fresh?

Down in Georgia, Dr. Crawford Long heard about the controversy and finally wrote an article in 1849. The simple fact was that he had been first. However, he admitted his "negligence" in not describing his work earlier and said that "with the decision which may be made, I shall be content."

It wasn't just a question of who would receive the glory. The U.S. Congress decided that because of anesthesia's importance its discoverer would receive a $100,000 prize—equivalent to $2 million in today's money.

Each of the four men had his boosters. Massachusetts General Hospital, site of his October 16, 1846, headline-making operation, favored Morton. Southerners generally favored Crawford Long. Northerners supported Wells, Morton, or Jackson. Dentists sided with Wells or Morton, doctors

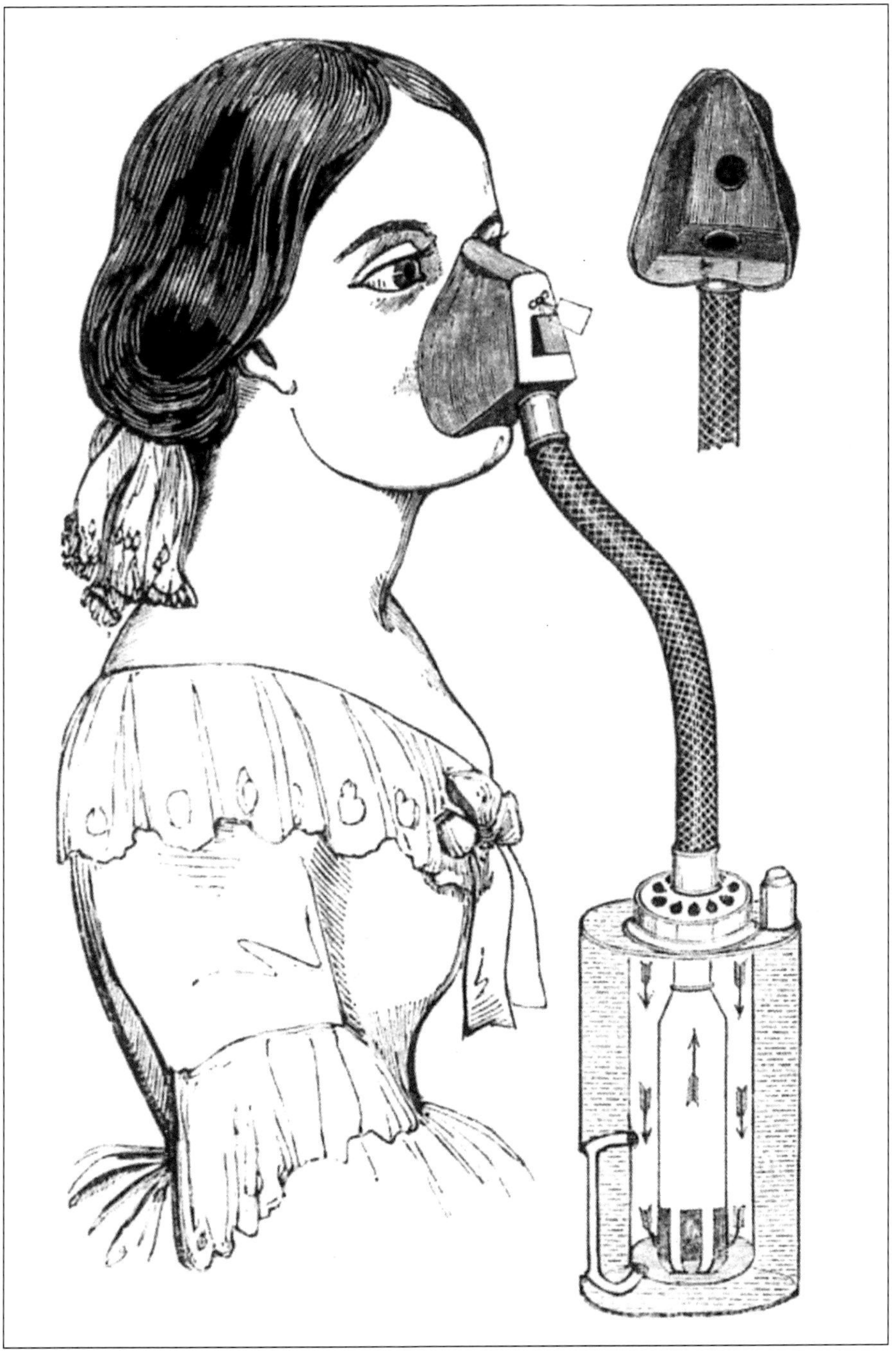

Young woman with early anesthesia inhaler.

with Long or Jackson, and geologists and chemists with Jackson. Pharmacists tended to line up behind Crawford Long, who, besides practicing medicine, had opened a drugstore in Athens, Georgia. Foreign countries also had their favorites and awarded medals and prizes to one man or another.

While under the influence of drugs, the dentist who had been known as a shy and sensitive soul became a madman.

The anesthesia controversy led to the deaths of three of the men. Horace Wells, who never got over his "failure" when the patient groaned, became addicted to breathing ether, nitrous oxide, and another anesthetic called chloroform. Scientists now know that inhaling drugs repeatedly over time can damage the brain. While under the influence of drugs, the dentist who had been known as a shy and sensitive soul became a madman. On his thirty-third birthday—January 21, 1848—Wells went out walking along Broadway in New York City. As he sneaked breaths from an anesthetic-filled bottle, his mind snapped. He sprinkled acid on two women and was locked in jail, where he killed himself on the morning of January 24, 1848. It is believed that his tragic story lives on in a famous novel by Robert Louis Stevenson. *The Strange Case of Dr. Jekyll and Mr. Hyde*—about a doctor who takes a drug that transforms him into a maniac—is believed to have been inspired by the last days of Horace Wells.

Morton gave up his dental practice and dedicated himself to winning the $100,000 government prize. In the process he shattered his nerves and fell $50,000 in debt. Morton sank so low that, to buy his family bread, he was forced to gather wood in the forest and sell it from a handcart. While in New York City to present his side of the story to magazines, Morton suffered an attack, perhaps a stroke, and died on the night of July 15, 1868, at the age of only forty-eight.

Jackson craved credit for the discovery rather than the monetary prize. He developed a strong hatred for Morton, whom he had advised about ether, and even took Long's side at times just to prevent Morton or Wells from receiving the credit. He intended to later point out that Long had waited too many years to publish his results, leaving Jackson standing alone as the acknowledged discoverer of anesthesia. In his frustration and jealousy of the other contenders, Jackson turned more and more to alcohol.

One day in July of 1873, Jackson drunkenly made his way to the cemetery outside Boston where William Morton was buried. He read the inscription that can still be seen on the impressive monument put up over the grave by some Bostonians:

WM. T.G. MORTON,

INVENTOR AND REVEALER OF ANESTHETIC INHALATION

Seeing Morton credited in death as the discoverer of anesthesia was more than Jackson could take. He went insane on the spot. He was taken away, kicking and screaming, and spent the last seven years of his life in an asylum, where he died in 1880 at the age of seventy-five.

Only Crawford Long, who had said he would accept "the decision which may be made," lived out a normal life. He and his wife had twelve children and shared an extremely happy home. On June 16, 1878, after delivering a baby, he suddenly felt ill and collapsed. His final words were, "Care for the mother and child first." Dr. Long, who had suffered a stroke, then died at the age of sixty-two.

Accidents and luck—people banging their shins under the influence of ether and laughing gas, a patient groaning at the wrong time, a dog knocking over a jar of ether—had played an important role in inspiring

Perhaps the only place the four contenders for the discovery of anesthesia appear together is in this painting at the International Museum of Surgical Science in Chicago; from left, Wells, Long, Jackson, and Morton.

the discovery of anesthesia. But the $100,000 was never awarded to anyone. When the Ether Monument honoring the discovery of anesthesia was placed in Boston's Public Garden in 1867, it didn't credit anyone in particular as the discoverer. Dr. Oliver Wendell Holmes, who coined the word *anesthesia*, joked that it should be inscribed TO E(I)THER.

Anesthesia did not save many lives at first. Surgical patients continued to die for reasons that puzzled doctors. Finally, in the 1870s, scientists discovered that germs were the problem. In the late 1800s antiseptic surgery, which involves killing germs, and aseptic surgery, which involves keeping them out of the operating room to start with, were introduced. These new methods allowed anesthesia to achieve its full potential, for deaths from germs had limited the usefulness of surgery almost as much as the threat of pain. The combination of anesthesia and germ-free surgery has allowed doctors to perform complex operations and to conquer conditions that were once considered hopeless.

So what is the final verdict—should we credit Long, Wells, Morton, or Jackson? That is a question you can decide for yourself, as medical historians continue to disagree over who should be considered the discoverer of anesthesia.

V Ignaz Semmelweis

Doctors, Wash Your Hands!

How would you like to go to a doctor or dentist who didn't wash his or her hands even once all day? What would you think of a surgeon who wore a bloodstained apron like a butcher, and who operated with filthy instruments?

Patients routinely encountered such conditions well into the 1800s. In fact, surgeons wore the same smock month after month and joked that a coat wasn't properly broken in until it could stand up from all the dried blood caked on it. Since nobody yet knew about the existence of germs, neither medical professionals nor their patients realized that disease was spread by unclean conditions. Partly due to a friend's death and partly through his own research, a little-known Hungarian physician pointed the way to cleanliness among doctors, nurses, and other health-care workers. Although he didn't discover germs, he deduced that *something* harmful lodged on dirty hands and instruments. His efforts led to the clean conditions we expect in modern hospitals and medical facilities.

Ignaz Philipp Semmelweis was born in what is now Budapest, Hungary, on July 1, 1818. The fifth in a family of ten children, Ignaz grew up in an apartment above his father's grocery, the White Elephant.

When Ignaz was a child, Hungary was ruled by Austria, a German-speaking empire. Ignaz was a lively and friendly boy, and a bright student. However, his education in the Budapest schools was deficient in one regard. He didn't learn to write in either Hungarian or German very well. As a result, he had a complex about his writing ability. In later years, this would have tragic repercussions.

In the autumn of 1837, nineteen-year-old Ignaz enrolled as a law student at the University of Vienna, in the capital of the Austrian Empire. He was studying law, in hope of becoming a military judge, when something

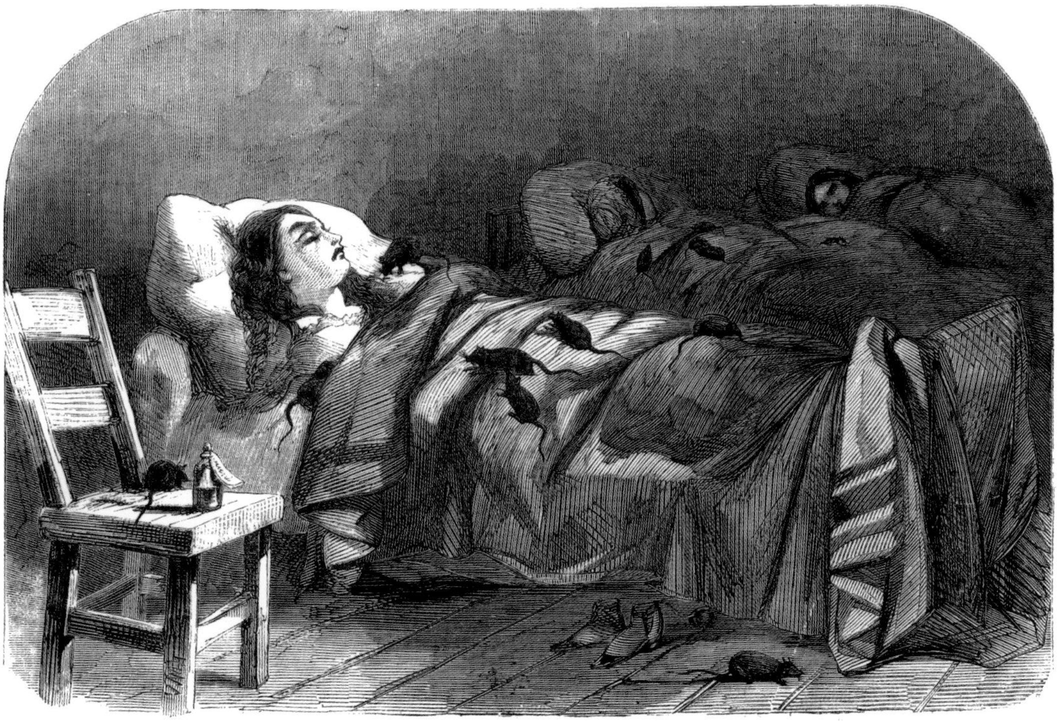

Before the twentieth century, hospitals were often dirty and overrun by rodents, as shown in this dramatic illustration of a New York City hospital in the 1800s.

unexpected occurred. A friend who was a medical student invited Semmelweis to attend an anatomy lesson. Ignaz intently watched the anatomy professor dissect a dead body in a foul-smelling room. Instead of being repulsed by the sights and smells, Ignaz was fascinated. He decided to abandon law and become a physician.

Ignaz studied medicine for about six years, and in 1844, at the age of twenty-five, he received his medical degree from the University of Vienna. He decided to specialize in obstetrics—the branch of medicine dealing with pregnancy and childbirth. After some additional study, he applied for a position as a doctor at the First Obstetrical Clinic of the Vienna General Hospital, widely considered to be the world's foremost teaching and research hospital. On July 1, 1846—his twenty-eighth birthday—Ignaz was hired to run the First Obstetrical Clinic.

Because of disease, the average life span in Semmelweis's day was only half of what it is today.

At the time, people were subject to an array of diseases that have since been brought under control. Because of disease, the average life span in Semmelweis's day was only half of what it is today. Perhaps Ignaz thought that delivering babies would be one of the pleasanter branches of medicine. It wasn't—at least not in the First Obstetrical Clinic of the Vienna General Hospital.

In the nineteenth century many new mothers died from a condition called *childbed fever*, also known as *puerperal fever* (from the Latin word *puerpera*, meaning "woman in childbirth"). Although some women who gave birth at home contracted it, childbed fever was especially prevalent in hospitals. The disease was fatal in over half the cases in which patients showed symptoms.

Between the 1660s and the 1860s there were about two hundred epidemics of childbed fever. One of the most severe lasted from 1773 to 1776 and killed more than a tenth of all women who gave birth in European hospitals. As late as the 1860s a three-year epidemic at the maternity hospital in Paris, France, killed *one out of five* of the new mothers. There were also major childbed fever epidemics in Boston, Massachusetts; London, England; Dublin, Ireland; Edinburgh, Scotland; Stockholm, Sweden; and many other cities.

Doctors didn't know what caused childbed fever, yet they put forth plenty of theories. Some thought that milk and other substances in a new mother's body brought about the illness. Others blamed changes in the weather or mysterious vapors in the air called miasmas. Still other physicians declared that new mothers contracted childbed fever because they were depressed, ate improperly, wore tight clothing, or didn't get enough exercise. Actually, childbed fever was an infection, which meant that it was caused by germs. More specifically, it was an infection of the placental site (the tissue connecting the mother to the baby) that often resulted in blood poisoning.

The disease was rampant in the Vienna General Hospital where Ignaz Semmelweis worked. Again and again a healthy woman in the prime of life entered the hospital, only to suffer fever, chills, and abdominal pains a few days after giving birth. The sickness often ended in her death. The veteran doctors on the staff thought that, like themselves, Ignaz would eventually accept childbed fever as inevitable in a certain number of cases. But Ignaz was a sensitive and gentle soul who was tormented each time a new childbed fever victim was borne away to the morgue. He vowed, as he later wrote, "to discover the mysterious agent" that caused childbed fever.

He began searching for clues. In 1840 the Vienna General Hospital's childbirth facilities had been divided into two divisions: the First Obstetrical Clinic, where Ignaz worked, and the Second Obstetrical Clinic. Among Vienna's expectant mothers, it was well known that the risk of childbed

Dr. Ignaz Semmelweis

fever was far greater in the first than in the second division. Ignaz wrote that he often "witnessed moving scenes in which patients, kneeling and wringing their hands, beg to be released in order to seek admission to the second section." Some women even preferred to have their babies in the streets rather than risk being admitted to the First Clinic.

Fortunately, the hospital kept excellent records, which enabled Ignaz to compare the two clinics. As he studied the hospital statistics, he saw that the women's dread of the First Clinic was no superstition. Year after year, it did have a higher mortality rate—sometimes *much* higher—than the Second Clinic:

Vienna General Hospital: Death Rate from Childbed Fever

Year	First Clinic	Second Clinic
1839	5.5 percent	4.5 percent
1840	9.5 percent	2.6 percent
1841	7.8 percent	3.5 percent
1842	15.8 percent	7.6 percent
1843	9 percent	6 percent
1844	8.2 percent	2.3 percent
1845	6.9 percent	2 percent
1846	11.4 percent	2.8 percent

On average, the First Clinic's death rate from childbed fever was nearly two and a half times that of the Second Clinic. In 1846, the year Ignaz went to work at the First Clinic, the mortality rate was four times that of the other clinic. Why?

Ignaz compared the two clinics in every way he could think of. The clinics were next to each other and even shared some of the same facilities, so it was not possible that the weather or mysterious vapors would affect one section and not the other. There was no reason to think that the patients in the First Clinic differed in diet, clothing, or exercise from the new mothers in the Second Clinic. Certainly the patients in the two clinics didn't differ in the milk or other substances that their bodies produced.

"I [was] like a drowning person grasping at straws," Ignaz later wrote. However, he did find several differences in the two sections. For one, expectant mothers in the First Clinic gave birth lying on their backs, while those in the Second Clinic had their babies from a lateral (sideways) position. Ignaz did not believe it would make any difference, but he ordered the First Clinic staff to deliver babies with the mothers in a lateral position.

As Ignaz had expected, changing the mother's position made no dent in the death rate.

With depressing regularity, the priest came from the hospital chapel to administer the last rites to childbed fever victims. The priest and his assistant, who accompanied him ringing a bell, could proceed directly to the dying women in the Second Clinic without passing through other rooms. On the other hand, the shortest route to the First Clinic's sickroom passed through several rooms filled with maternity patients. Ignaz's heart sank every time he heard the bell ringing. Could the frequent appearance of the priest and the tolling of the bell upset the women enough to make them susceptible to childbed fever? It seemed unlikely, but, wanting to look at every possibility, Ignaz asked the priest to come without bells, and to take a less direct route to the sickroom. "Thus," he wrote, "no one outside the room containing the ill patients knew of the priest's presence."

Ignaz wasn't surprised that the death rate remained unchanged.

Perhaps the biggest difference was in the staff of the two clinics. In the Second Clinic, female midwives delivered the babies and cared for the mothers. In the First Clinic, female midwives generally delivered the babies, but doctors and medical students, who were all male, examined the women before and after they gave birth. Might the female midwives somehow be better for the maternity patients than the male doctors and medical students? At first, Ignaz didn't think that was possible. Like other physicians of the time, he believed that doctors and medical students, who were more formally educated than the midwives, did a better job of caring for the new mothers.

[Ignaz] was so obsessed with childbed fever that he hardly slept.

Day after day, Ignaz studied the statistics, read books and articles to learn other doctors' opinions, and went over the problem endlessly in his mind. He was so obsessed with childbed fever that he hardly slept. Early each morning, before beginning his duties in the First Clinic, he entered the hospital morgue and dissected the dead bodies of the latest childbed fever victims. Still, he found no clues as to why the disease was so prevalent in the First Clinic.

Another factor made the situation even more puzzling. Sometimes newborn babies, like their mothers, died of what seemed to be childbed fever. These infants hadn't been in the world long enough to be affected by any of the factors that supposedly caused childbed fever. What was killing the babies?

Lajos Markusovszky, a close friend of his, later recalled Ignaz's frustration during this period. Markusovszky wrote:

> *Thanks to his kindness, I was sharing rooms with Semmelweis. I had the chance of seeing him, both in the hospital and at home: his watchful restlessness, his eagerness to examine patients and conditions, his prying eyes trying to penetrate into the murderous disease, his zest to discover its cause. He left nothing unex-*

> *plored. Semmelweis examined the new patients coming into the clinic most thoroughly, prescribed their diets, made women in labor lie on their side, as was the habit in the 2nd Clinic. After delivery they were carried to the wards so that they should not be compelled to walk as heretofore. He [studied] records of all who had died in the hospital. He devoted special care to cleanliness and ventilation and even persuaded the clergyman to administer the Last Sacrament to the dying by going straight to the bed without making a detour in the hospital. All in vain! The death bell kept ringing in spite of all precautions and deeply distressed Semmelweis.*

Ignaz suffered another blow. Johannes Klein, the director of the hospital's two maternity units, did not like him. Dr. Klein felt that by snooping into the records and dwelling on the large number of deaths in the First Clinic, Ignaz was placing the hospital in a bad light. In the fall of 1846 Klein seized the chance to get rid of Semmelweis. The doctor who ran the First Clinic before Ignaz wanted his old position back. Dr. Klein replaced Ignaz with this man. After just four months of running the First Clinic, Ignaz was out of work. The timing was particularly bad for Ignaz because his father had recently died.

Semmelweis began studying English in hope of finding a position in an English-speaking country. He remained unemployed for just a few months, though. The doctor who had replaced him soon left to become a professor at a university in Germany, and in early 1847 Ignaz was rehired in his old position. But before returning to work, he decided to take what would be the only vacation of his life. In March of 1847 Ignaz traveled to Venice (in what is now Italy) with his friend Lajos Markusovszky, "in order," he wrote, "to refresh my depressed spirits that had been very much tried by the events in the clinic."

On March 20, 1847, Ignaz returned to Vienna and immediately resumed his work in the First Clinic. Some tragic news dampened his return. His friend and colleague Dr. Jakob Kolletschka had died in his absence. What had happened to end the forty-three-year-old medical professor's life so unexpectedly? Jakob had been dissecting a dead body with a group of students when suddenly his finger had been pricked by a student's medical knife. The wound had become inflamed, and Dr. Jakob Kolletschka soon died. This chance event provided the clue Ignaz had been seeking. For as he read the report on his friend's death, Ignaz came to a startling realization. He later wrote:

The wound had become inflamed, and Dr. Jakob Kolletschka soon died. This chance event provided the clue Ignaz had been seeking.

> *I could see clearly that the disease from which Kolletschka died was identical to that from which so many hundreds of new mothers had also died. The cause of Professor Kolletschka's death was known. It was the wound by the knife that had been contaminated by particles from the dead body. The particles caused his death. I had to admit that if his disease was identical with the disease that killed so many maternity patients, then it must have originated from the same cause that brought it on in Kolletschka.*

The medical students and doctors of the First Clinic, including Ignaz Semmelweis, often dissected dead bodies and then examined the new mothers without washing their hands. Apparently material from the dead bodies remained on their hands and infected the new mothers, just as the contaminated knife had infected Jakob Kolletschka. Germs weren't yet known, so Ignaz didn't realize that they were the culprits. Still, he knew that something unclean on the doctors' and students' hands was giving the women childbed fever.

Everything now made sense. The death rate was lower in the Second Clinic because the midwives who cared for the new mothers there did not dissect dead bodies. Ignaz was horrified to realize that *he* had been a cause of the First Clinic's high death rate for 1846. In the hope that it would help him understand childbed fever, he had dissected many bodies. But instead of saving lives, he had carried death to many new mothers on his hands! Was it possible that simply by washing their hands thoroughly, medical workers could prevent childbed fever?

The death rate was lower in the Second Clinic because the midwives who cared for the new mothers there did not dissect dead bodies.

Washing just with soap and water wouldn't be sufficient, Ignaz knew. After he left the dissecting room, the stink from the cadavers (dead bodies) remained on his hands even after washing with soap and water. A stronger disinfectant was needed to remove the cadaverous poison from the hands. Ignaz experimented with various substances and settled on a solution of chloride of lime as a reliable disinfectant. In late May of 1847—just two months after his return from Venice—Ignaz ordered everyone in the First Clinic to wash thoroughly with this solution before beginning their rounds. However, Ignaz thought it was sufficient for the staff to wash only with soap and water between patients.

The results were stunning and immediate. The First Clinic's death rate from childbed fever had been 11.4 percent in 1846. The 1847 death rate dropped to 2.4 percent in June, 1.2 percent in July, and 1.9 percent in August. In fact, the First Clinic's mortality rate dropped below that of the Second Clinic! The tragic death of Jakob Kolletschka, and Ignaz Semmelweis's careful analysis of it, had resulted in a discovery that could save countless lives. All that medical workers had to do was wash their hands carefully with an effective disinfectant to dramatically reduce the mortality rate from childbed fever. This would also reduce the death rate among infants, many of whom contracted the disease from their mothers.

In late summer the First Clinic's death rate rose again. Ignaz did more detective work and figured out why. Annoyed that the cleansing solution irritated their hands, some students had ignored Dr. Semmelweis's order and had neglected to wash. Ignaz, for whom combating childbed fever had become his mission in life, gave them a tongue-lashing. He also put up signs stating which medical personnel were assigned to each patient. That way he could track down anyone who tended to spread infections.

Nevertheless, disaster struck in October when eleven out of twelve maternity patients in one room died of childbed fever. A patient with an

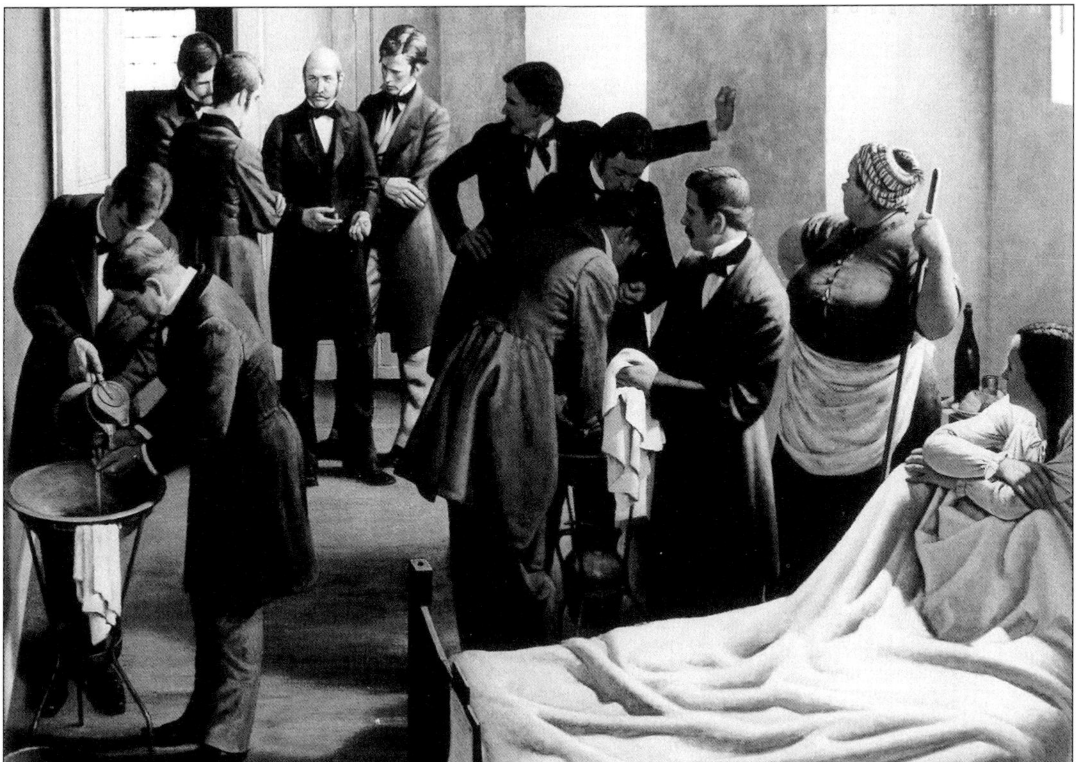

Artist's version of hand washing as initiated by Dr. Ignaz Semmelweis, who is the balding man facing us at upper left.

oozing cancer had been in the room with these women, Ignaz discovered. The staff had always examined the cancer patient first, then washed their hands with soap and water as Ignaz had ordered before examining each of the new mothers. Evidently poisons from the cancer had been spread into the healthy women, infecting them with childbed fever. This proved that childbed fever could result from other kinds of decaying matter besides poisons from dead bodies. It also showed that it wasn't enough for the staff to wash with the disinfectant solution once in the morning and then wash only with soapy water between patients. They must wash with the disinfectant solution after each and every patient, Ignaz ordered.

November brought another tragic lesson. This time a woman with an infected knee spread childbed fever to other patients in her ward. Since the staff hadn't touched the woman's knee, apparently the infection had traveled through the air. After that, Semmelweis made sure that patients who were already ill with infections were isolated from the healthy patients.

By late 1847 accounts of Ignaz Semmelweis's discovery were making their way across Europe. Ignaz and several of his students wrote letters to a number of maternity clinics. Ferdinand Hebra, a prominent skin doctor at the Vienna General Hospital, wrote an article about Ignaz's discovery that appeared in the December 1847 Vienna medical society *Journal*, and another article that appeared in the *Journal* the following April. The year 1848 brought more proof for Semmelweis's theory. That year the death rate from childbed fever in the First Clinic dipped to 1.27 percent, slightly less than that of the Second Clinic, which also seems to have adopted his methods to some extent. Only about one in every hundred new mothers was dying of childbed fever in the First Clinic, compared to more than eleven out of every hundred two years before.

A few prominent obstetricians embraced Ignaz's theory and adopted his hand-washing method. They included Dr. Gustav Michaelis of Kiel, Germany. After instituting the chloride of lime washings, there had been only one case of childbed fever in his clinic over a period of several months, Dr. Michaelis reported. But his acceptance of the Semmelweis theory was accompanied by a sorrowful realization for Dr. Michaelis. Not long before starting the hand-washing technique, Dr. Michaelis had delivered a baby for his cousin, who had become ill with childbed fever and died. Convinced that she had contracted the disease from his hands, Dr. Gustav Michaelis committed suicide by throwing himself under a train.

Ignaz had assumed that his measures for preventing childbed fever would spread rapidly around the world. After all, hand washing was so simple.

Ignaz had assumed that his measures for preventing childbed fever would spread rapidly around the world. After all, hand washing was so simple. Had he written a book in 1849 or 1850, his doctrine might have been universally adopted within a short time. But Ignaz, who once confessed to an "inborn dislike for everything that can be called writing," did not produce a book for many years, opening the way for doctors to criticize or ignore his doctrine.

He was opposed on several counts. Doctors asked: What was the mysterious something on their hands that spread childbed fever? Since germs weren't yet known, Ignaz had no answer. Also, Ignaz was one of the first medical researchers to make his point through statistics (the mathematical collection and analysis of data), which few doctors of the 1840s trusted. There was another problem. Physicians were reluctant to admit that *they* were spreading disease, for that would leave them open to the kind of guilt Dr. Michaelis had suffered.

To make things worse, Ignaz received little support from his hospital and was actually opposed by his boss, Dr. Johannes Klein. It wasn't just that Semmelweis had made the Vienna General Hospital's past record look bad. In 1848–1849, Hungary revolted against the Austrian Empire but was defeated. As a result, Hungarians such as Ignaz Semmelweis were resented in Austria. Had Ignaz been Austrian, his doctrine might have been quickly accepted and thousands of lives might have been saved.

In the fall of 1850 Ignaz was forced out of the Vienna General Hospital, due mainly to Dr. Johannes Klein. Semmelweis returned to his birthplace, Budapest. There he found work at hospitals and at the university and expanded upon his theory. It wasn't just important to clean medical workers' hands, he determined. Instruments, bed linen, and everything else that came into contact with maternity patients must be clean. As in Vienna, he dramatically reduced the death rate from childbed fever.

Back in his birthplace, Ignaz found more happiness than he had ever known before. In 1857, at the age of thirty-nine, he married a young Budapest woman, Maria Weidenhoffer, with whom he would have five children. At about that time he finally picked up his pen.

Ignaz wrote an account of his work in an essay published in 1858. To his surprise, once he got started, writing was not as difficult as he had feared. He began writing a longer work, and once he started, he couldn't stop. His 543-page book, *The Etiology, Concept, and Prophylaxis of Childbed Fever*, was published in October of 1860. (*Etiology* means "cause," and *prophylaxis* refers to preventing the spread of disease.) Page by page, he presented all the facts, statistics, and observations he had accumulated for over a decade. "It would be a crime to remain silent any longer," he explained. Pleading with doctors to adopt his cleanliness methods, he declared that "my doctrine is produced to banish terror from the maternity hospitals, to preserve the wife to the husband, the mother to the child."

Unfortunately, during the thirteen years since he had first formed his theory, many doctors had become even more entrenched in the belief that atmospheric disturbances or miasmas caused childbed fever. Ignaz's book was generally ignored or ridiculed.

Ignaz Semmelweis then decided to take on his opponents one by one in a letter-writing war. Ignaz was compelled to do so because "the groaning of the women dying of childbed fever is louder than the beating of my heart," he wrote in one letter. "There is no other course open to me but to put an end to the murderous practices of my adversaries by exposing them. Everyone with a feeling heart will understand that there is no other course open to me."

"The groaning of the women dying of childbed fever is louder than the beating of my heart."

As his frustration grew, Ignaz accused doctors who refused to wash their hands of perpetrating "murderous practices," "massacres," and "homicides." All he seemed to talk or think about was childbed fever. By 1865 his wife, Maria, and his friends believed he was losing his mind. That summer Ignaz was confined to an insane asylum in Vienna.

Treatment of the mentally ill was terrible in those days. Instead of being helped, Ignaz was severely beaten by asylum guards. His wounds became badly infected. On August 13, 1865, forty-seven-year-old Ignaz Semmelweis died of blood poisoning—the very disease he had fought to conquer in maternity patients.

Ignaz Semmelweis had written in his book: "Should it not be my fate to see with my own eyes the happy future" when childbed fever would be conquered, "the firm belief that this time will come will cheer my dying hour."

The time *did* come when his theory was finally accepted. During the 1870s Louis Pasteur of France and Robert Koch of Germany showed that germs cause disease. Suddenly it was clear why doctors with filthy hands spread childbed fever, for germs, also called microorganisms or microbes, thrived in unclean conditions.

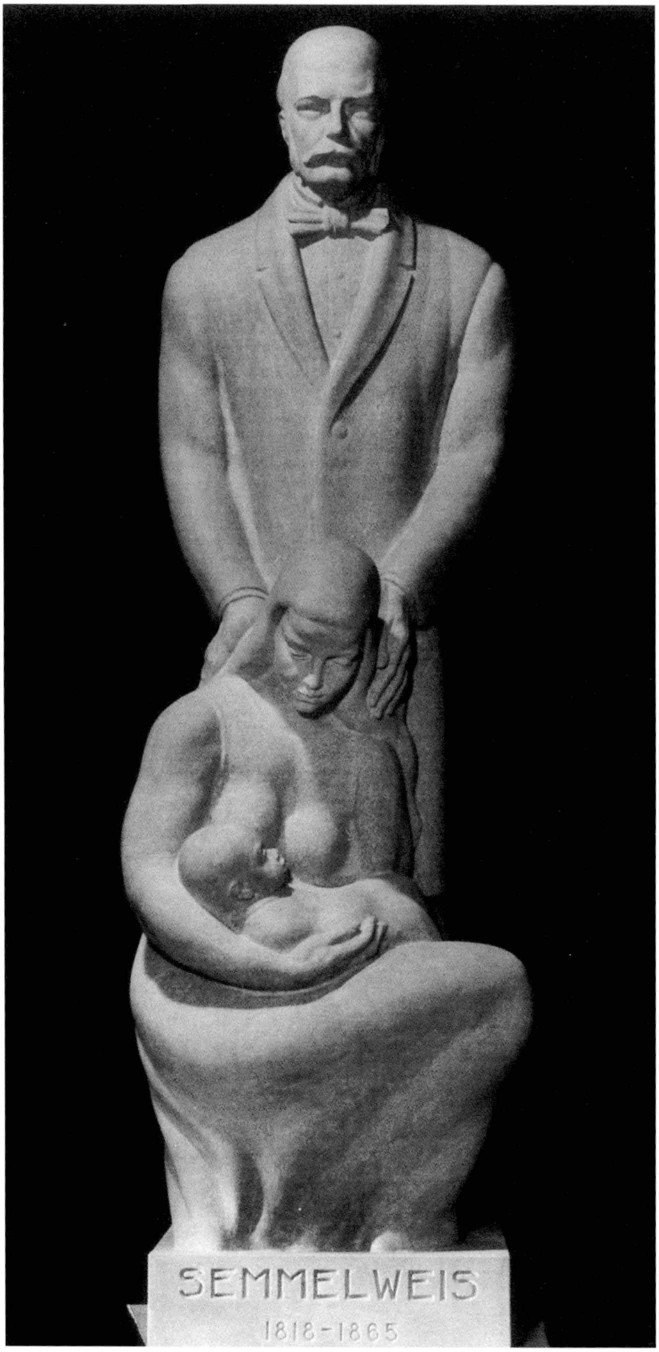

This statue of Dr. Ignaz Semmelweis with a mother and newborn baby is at the International Museum of Surgical Science in Chicago.

By the late 1800s there was a movement in developed countries to promote hygiene or cleanliness. Doctors, nurses, and medical facilities took precautions to maintain a clean environment, as did the public. Surgeons learned how to keep germs out of operating rooms and to kill any germs that might get in anyway. Washing and other methods of cleanliness that Ignaz Semmelweis had suggested were the main reason why life expectancy in the United States rose from less than forty years of age to almost fifty years between 1850 and 1900.

But what about the new mothers who, despite precautions, developed childbed fever? What about the men, women, and children who developed blood poisoning for various reasons? In the early and mid-1900s, medical researchers developed antibiotics that could cure these and other infections. The first of these "wonder drugs" was penicillin. How penicillin was discovered with a little bit of luck and some careful observation will be described in a later chapter.

VI Maria Sanz de Sautuola

The Bulls on the Ceiling

According to an old saying, "Curiosity killed the cat." Yet many discoveries have been made by people with a healthy curiosity—especially when they were helped along by a little good fortune. Curiosity helped an eight-year-old girl in Spain find something extremely unusual. In fact, what she came across was so unusual that for many years the world refused to accept her discovery as real.

Maria Sanz de Sautuola was born in or near the city of Santander in northern Spain on November 30, 1870. She was the only child of a wealthy nobleman, Marcelino Sanz de Sautuola, and his wife, Concepcion de Escalante. But Maria's story actually began two years before her birth with the disappearance of a dog.

In 1868 a man and his dog were hunting on an estate near Santander owned by Maria's parents. Suddenly the dog vanished, although the hunter could still hear him barking. Upon investigating, the hunter discovered

Photograph of Maria Sanz de Sautuola taken at about the time of her discovery.

that the animal had fallen into a crack in a hillside. The hunter rescued his dog, then cleared away the branches and dirt that covered the crack. The man realized that the opening was actually the mouth of a cave that had been covered by debris for untold centuries. He informed Marcelino Sanz de Sautuola that he had a cave on his property.

At first Maria's father had little interest in the crack on his hillside, for the mountains of northern Spain contained numerous caves. Not until 1875, when Maria was about five years old, did her father remove the debris from the entrance and begin to explore the cave.

In 1877 Maria's father traveled to Paris, France, where he attended a conference of archaeologists—scientists who study the remains of human cultures of the past. The archaeologists spoke about some extremely old skeletons that were found a few years earlier in France's Cro-Magnon Cave. The skeletons had come from people who lived in Europe, Africa, and Asia between 40,000 and 10,000 years ago. These prehistoric human beings were named the Cro-Magnon people, for the cave in which their skeletons were first discovered.

After her father returned from Paris, Maria listened to him talk about the cave people of long ago. She wondered: Might prehistoric people have lived in *their* cave? Her father was wondering the same thing. The only way to find out, he said, was to dig up the ground inside the cave.

Maria's father entered the cave with a candle and shovel and began digging a short way from the entrance. Maria must have asked to help, for soon she was accompanying him into the cave. Sometimes the pretty six-year-old girl with bright brown eyes and short brown hair held the candles so that her father could see where to dig. And sometimes he let her scoop out dirt with a small shovel.

According to notes made by Marcelino Sanz de Sautuola, within a year or so he and Maria had dug down to a depth of thirty centimeters, or one foot. They uncovered stone tools and pottery fragments, indicating that the cave had once been home to prehistoric people. They also found shells and animal bones, showing that the cave dwellers made trips to the nearby seashore and hunted for food.

Maria liked helping her father, but as the months passed, she grew bored with digging near the cave entrance, where the ancient people had built their fires and lived. Her eyes began to wander toward the dark recesses of the cave, where she and her father had never explored. Again and again she almost asked him if she could go off exploring by herself, but as she stared into the blackness she couldn't quite summon the courage.

"Toros! Toros!" she shouted, for there, painted upon the ceiling, were pictures of what appeared to be bulls and other animals.

On a summer day in 1879, the father and daughter were digging at their usual spot near the mouth of the cave. Once more Maria's eyes wandered into the darkness. By now her curiosity must have outweighed her fear, for she finally asked if she could take a candle and go deeper into the cave by herself. Yes, her father said, but she must not stray too far.

The eight-year-old girl began walking slowly through the passage. As weird shapes cast by her candle's flame leaped out at her from the walls and ceiling, she felt the urge to run back to her father. But Maria's curiosity spurred her on until she arrived in a kind of large hall.

For a few moments Maria looked about the huge chamber. Then something above her head caught her attention. "*Toros! Toros!*" she shouted, for there, painted upon the ceiling, were pictures of what appeared to be bulls and other animals. In the flickering candlelight the animals seemed to be running along the ceiling as they stared down at her.

Her father heard Maria's shouts echoing through the cave. Although he couldn't imagine why Maria was yelling about bulls, he immediately ran toward his daughter to protect her. He found Maria in the large chamber gazing not at real bulls but at lovely paintings. What she had called bulls were actually pictures of bison. Maria and her father counted paintings of fifteen bison, as well as pictures of three deer, two horses, three wild boars, and a wolf.

Prehistoric people must have created the paintings, Maria's father said. When she asked why the paintings looked fresh, he explained that until the dog had stumbled upon the cave, it had been sealed, keeping the air out. But scientists would have to come to make certain of the great age of the cave art.

Maria's father wrote letters inviting archaeologists to come and see the cave paintings. Only Professor Juan de Vilanova y Piera, of Spain's capital city of Madrid, agreed to come. When the professor arrived, Maria and

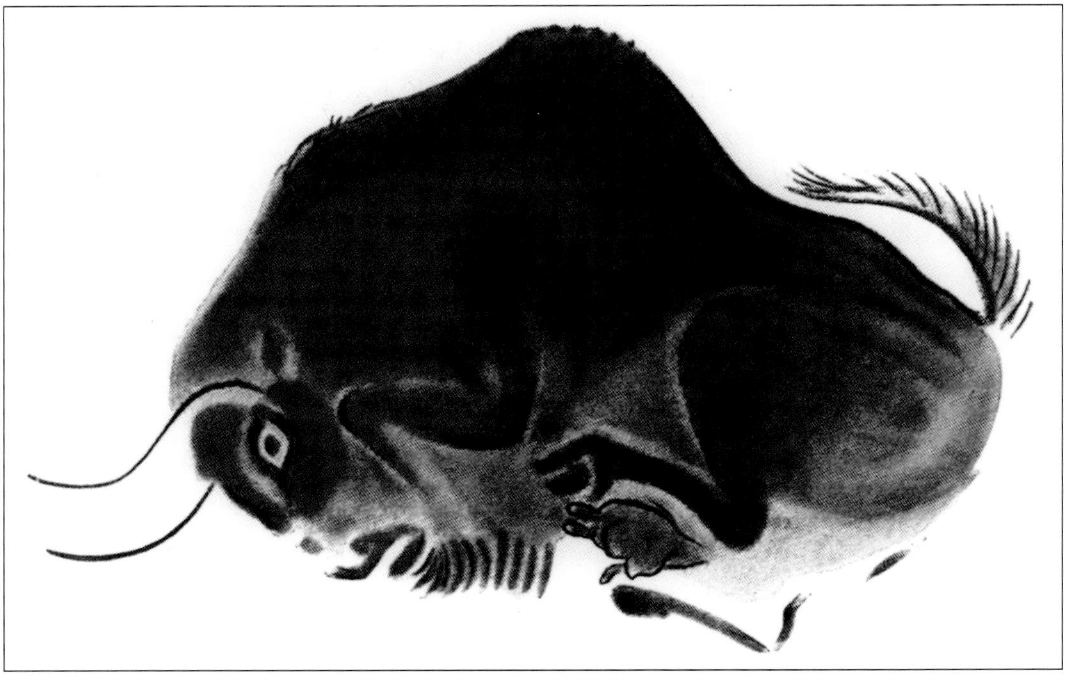

One of the bison paintings at the Cave of Altamira.

her father led him out to the hillside and into the cave. Professor Vilanova studied the cave paintings and listened to the story of how Maria found them. Then he said that Maria had made a most important discovery. She had discovered the world's first known cave paintings made by ancient human beings. The paintings were made by Cro-Magnon people and were roughly 15,000 years old, the professor correctly believed. The bison were a clue, for such animals hadn't lived in Spain for more than 12,000 years.

A young girl's curiosity had resulted in a great discovery.

Maria hadn't just found the world's oldest known paintings, Professor Vilanova continued. Archaeologists had pictured cave people as club-wielding savages who lacked the "finer feelings" we modern human beings claim to possess. The paintings proved that Cro-Magnon people had an appreciation for beauty. Also, the cave artists had gone into a separate chamber to paint, just as modern artists usually seek privacy. All this meant that in certain basic ways human beings hadn't changed over a period of 15,000 years.

Professor Vilanova's conclusions were accurate. A young girl's curiosity had resulted in a great discovery. Of course good fortune played a role, too, for the cave happened to be one of relatively few containing prehistoric art. Because of its location in a meadow named *Altamira*, meaning "High View" in Spanish, the cavern became known as the Cave of Altamira. Journalists in Spain nicknamed Maria "the Girl of Altamira." For a brief, joyful period, the Girl of Altamira and her father were hailed across their homeland.

The leading archaeologists at that time were in France, however. Only if the French scientists approved the discovery would it be accepted throughout the world. Maria's father and Professor Vilanova wrote letters to the French scientists, inviting them to visit the Cave of Altamira. Months passed and not one French scientist accepted the invitation.

The problem was that a famous French archaeologist named Emile Cartailhac wouldn't consider the possibility that the paintings were thousands of years old. Cave people were incapable of beautiful artwork, he declared. Besides, he asserted, cave paintings couldn't possibly last for thousands of years.

They accused her father of paying the artist to paint the cave pictures so that Maria and her family would become famous.

The French archaeologists ridiculed Marcelino Sanz de Sautuola's claim for another reason. It happened that, during the summer of the discovery, an artist had been in the region where Maria's family lived. He came to touch up old family portraits belonging to people in the area, but the French scientists didn't believe that. They accused her father of paying the artist to paint the cave pictures so that Maria and her family would become famous. So certain were Emile Cartailhac and his colleagues of their conclusions that they refused to come see the paintings.

No longer were there newspaper stories praising the Girl of Altamira and her father. Instead, Marcelino was branded a "faker" and a "liar." His spirits were crushed. Maria sadly watched as he wrote letter after letter, practically begging the French archaeologists to visit the Cave of Altamira. He even began following the archaeologists around to their meetings. In 1880 he made a journey to an archaeologists' conference at Lisbon, Portugal, where he distributed copies of a pamphlet he had written about the cave paintings. But the scientists ignored his booklet and made fun of Maria's father. He returned home brokenhearted, telling his wife and daughter that he had been treated with "*indiferencia y desprecio*" (indifference and scorn).

Marcelino Sanz de Sautuola never recovered from being called a liar. He walked about the grounds of his estate for hours at a time, lost in thought. In the middle of the night he went out to the cave to look at the paintings by candlelight. He continued to ask the archaeologists to visit the cave, but they began to consider him somewhat deranged on the subject. Maria wanted to help, but she was still a child, so what could she do? Her father died in 1888 at the age of just fifty-seven. Today's doctors might say that he had suffered a heart attack or stroke, but his wife and daughter were convinced that he had died of what the family called an "enormous sorrow."

Professor Vilanova died in 1893. With the passing of the only scientist who had believed the paintings were genuine, the cause seemed hopeless. Maria continued to write letters to the French archaeologists with no more success than her father had achieved. Maria and her mother also decided

The metal gate Maria and her mother put up to safeguard the entrance of the cave.

that the great artworks in the Cave of Altamira must be preserved for the sake of Marcelino and for future generations. They constructed a large metal gate to block the entrance of the cave. Maria hid the key, vowing that she wouldn't unlock the gate until the professors came to admit their mistake.

As the years passed, Maria became a beautiful young woman. She liked to dance and attend balls that she and her friends held at one another's homes. In the spring of 1895, at the age of twenty-four, Maria married. She and her husband later had five children. Maria's son Emilio Botin supplied much of the information for this chapter when he was in his eighties.

About the time that Maria married, a group of boys discovered some cave paintings in France. Over the next few years additional cave art was found in Europe. Professor Cartailhac and the other French archaeologists were forced to admit that prehistoric people resembled us much more than they had believed. They also remembered how, many years earlier, a man named Marcelino Sanz de Sautuola had written a pamphlet and followed them around, claiming that his daughter had discovered prehistoric cave paintings in northern Spain.

One day in 1902, Maria received a letter from France. Professor Emile Cartailhac wanted to visit the Cave of Altamira and have Maria show him the paintings. Now in her thirties, Maria wrote back saying that she had been awaiting his letter for many years.

Soon after, Professor Cartailhac paid Maria a visit. He was accompanied by Henri Breuil, a French priest who was also an expert on prehistoric people. Maria took the key from her hiding place. She led the two scientists up the hill and unlocked the gate that she and her mother had constructed at the cave's entrance. Much as she had done as an eight-year-old child, Maria carried a candle to light the way into the cave's great hall. With the professors at her side, Maria gazed up at the bulls on the ceiling, just as she had on a summer day twenty-three years earlier.

It was said that when he looked up at the ceiling, Professor Cartailhac dropped to his knees in shame and begged Maria to forgive him in her father's name. He knew he had wronged an honest man, for the paintings were similar to ancient cave art that had since been discovered in France. Emilio Botin recalled that, during his childhood, "My mother told me many times about how the French Professor Cartailhac asked her for forgiveness when he came to visit."

When he looked up at the ceiling, Professor Cartailhac dropped to his knees in shame and begged Maria to forgive him in her father's name.

But it wasn't enough for Professor Cartailhac to apologize to her in the dark and lonely cave, Maria felt. He must put his apology in writing for all the world to see forever. Upon his return to France, Cartailhac wrote "My Mistake," an article in which he acknowledged that Maria Sanz de Sautuola had found the first known prehistoric cave paintings while excavating the Cave of Altamira with her father.

The paintings in the Cave of Altamira became famous as one of the great wonders of the prehistoric world. Many people, including King Alfonzo XIII of Spain, have come to marvel at the 15,000-year-old paintings, and to learn about their young discoverer and her father.

Maria lived to the age of seventy-five. She enjoyed showing her children and grandchildren articles and books that mentioned the Girl of Altamira and her father. Like other grandparents, she also told young members of her family bedtime stories. Only instead of fairy tales, Maria told them the story of how, at the age of eight, she found the bulls in the cave.

vii Alexander Fleming

Discoverer of Penicillin

One day in early September of 1928, Alexander Fleming returned to work after a month-long holiday, as they call a vacation in England. Alexander was a medical researcher at St. Mary's Hospital in London. Upon entering, he saw that his laboratory was a mess—just as he had left it and precisely how he liked it. The room was cluttered with such items as test tubes, microscopes, and slides; there were incubators for cultivating microbes, a sterilizer for cleaning instruments, various experiments, and a large number of petri dishes—shallow plates used for growing bacteria. His colleagues, as well as the maintenance workers, knew better than to clean up Dr. Fleming's laboratory in his absence. A firm believer that discoveries were more likely to occur in a laboratory with lots of activity than in a neat environment, Fleming was known for his love of disorder. Whenever someone suggested that he throw something out, his stock answer was: "Just put it aside. It may come in useful."

However, just to have enough room to work, even Dr. Fleming had to tidy up his laboratory occasionally. On the September day when

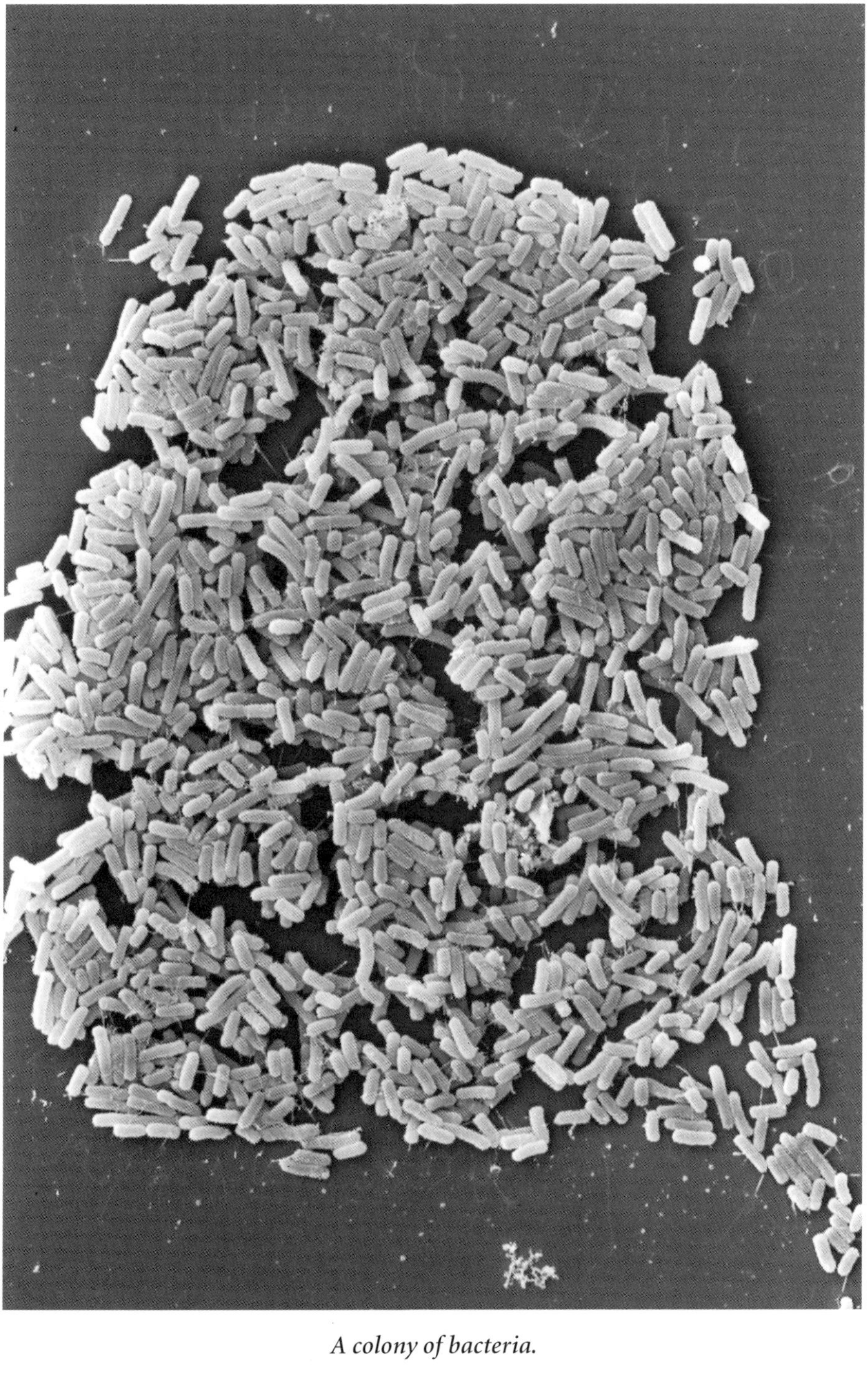

A colony of bacteria.

he returned from his vacation, he decided to clean some petri dishes that he had left piled on his workbench. In these plates he had grown colonies of staphylococci bacteria—germs that can cause pimples, skin infections, blood poisoning, and pneumonia. Fleming obtained his initial staphylococci supply from pimples and throat infections. He then grew colonies of staphylococci in his petri dishes to test whether variations in color indicated the harmfulness of the germs. With this phase of his experiment complete, he began cleaning the dishes with a disinfectant.

Fleming was very excited, but at this point he had more questions than answers.

In keeping with his belief that everything in the laboratory should be studied to see if it might "come in useful," Fleming examined each petri dish before disinfecting it. He was "doing the dishes" when Merlin Pryce, his former assistant, entered the room. Fleming pointed out to Pryce that some of the petri dishes had developed mold—a kind of fungus that grows on damp or decaying organic matter. Fleming was lightheartedly complaining about all the work he had to do since Pryce had transferred to another department when he noticed something strange.

"That's funny," he said, showing Pryce a moldy plate. Near the mold, the colonies of staphylococci bacteria had dissolved. It appeared that the mold somehow destroyed the germs.

Fleming was very excited, but at this point he had more questions than answers. There are thousands of kinds of molds, including those that live on damp bread, on cheeses, and in the soil. Which particular mold had landed on this plate? Did the mold really kill the staphylococci bacteria, or was there another explanation? If the mold destroyed the germs, might it be made into a medicine that could cure staphylococci infections? Might it also be effective against other germs? Had he just discovered the wonder drug that he and other medical researchers dreamed about?

Alexander Fleming was born on August 6, 1881, in a secluded farmhouse four miles from the town of Darvel in southwestern Scotland. Alec, as he was called, was the seventh in a family of eight sons and daughters. With the nearest neighbors about a mile away, Alec and his brothers and sisters learned to amuse themselves. They roamed their beautiful region of hills and valleys, climbed through waterfalls, fished in the streams, and bathed in the natural pools of water near their home. They also made up games, some of which were pretty rough. One day Alec was playing a game to see who could roll down a hillside the fastest. He picked a steep slope that ended with a sheer drop into a rocky gully. The other children watched in horror as Alec bounced toward the edge of the cliff. Fortunately—for himself and for humanity—he came to a stop just as he was about to plunge over the edge. Shaken by his close call, he said to the other children: "I came down *quick*!"

When Alec was six, his father suffered a stroke that left him an invalid. Later Alec remembered his father as a kindly, gray-haired man who couldn't move from his chair by the fireplace. He lived only a year following his stroke.

With his father gone, Alec had to help with the farmwork. He gathered hay, milked the cows, and tended his family's sheep. Sometimes when snowstorms completely covered the sheep with drifts he would have to find the animals quickly to rescue them. Alec learned to locate the sheep by looking for holes with yellow stains around them in the snowdrifts. These were telltale signs that the animals were struggling to breathe beneath the snow.

Alec had begun school at the age of five. Each day he walked a mile to the little school, where children of all ages were taught in a single classroom. On nice days the teacher held class outdoors along the riverbank.

Occasionally while outside they would see the school inspector approaching in his buggy. Teacher and pupils would then run to the school and climb in through a back window. They would all be in their proper places—albeit out of breath—by the time the school inspector entered the classroom.

When he was ten years old, Alec transferred to a larger school in Darvel, which was a four-mile walk each way. On cold winter mornings his mother would give Alec two freshly baked potatoes to keep in his pockets for his long walk to school. Alec would warm his hands on the potatoes, and then eat them for lunch.

Alec said that he learned to be observant during his long walks to and from school.

Later in life Alec said that he learned to be observant during his long walks to and from school. He discovered how to predict the weather from changes in the sky. He loved birds and taught himself to recognize their calls and songs. Flowers, trees, rocks, streams—everything in the countryside fascinated him.

Alec's oldest brother, who was seventeen years older than he, took over the family farm. Other family members decided to seek fame and fortune in London. Tom, thirteen years older than Alec, was the first to settle in London. He became a physician specializing in eye problems. Brother John followed and went to work for a firm that made eyeglasses. In 1895, thirteen-year-old Alec also went to London to live. His younger brother Robert arrived soon after. Their sister Mary kept house for the four brothers, making a total of five Fleming children living together in London.

Life there was different from anything Alec had ever known. The world's biggest city, London was a crowded, noisy place where there were more people in a single block than Alec had ever seen back home. The Flemings lived above the Metropolitan underground railway, and every few minutes their house shook as trains sped by beneath them.

London in the 1890s, when Alexander Fleming went there to live.

For about two years Alec attended London's Regent Street Polytechnic School, where he studied in preparation for a business career. At sixteen he left school and went to work as a clerk in a steamship company office. In those days before modern photocopy machines, his job was to make copies of letters and documents by hand, and to do other paperwork. He found the work boring, with little chance for advancement.

Treating patients was not his favorite part of medicine. What he liked best was experimenting.

In 1899 war broke out between the British and the Boers, who were South African people of Dutch heritage. Early the next year, eighteen-year-old Alec enlisted as a private in the London Scottish Regiment and began training on weekends and evenings while still working in the shipping office. At less than five feet six inches in height, Alec was small, but he was wiry and tough from spending much of his childhood outdoors. Army training came rather easily to him, even when his unit made a sixty-mile march in a downpour. He also enjoyed the shooting contests and rough sports the trainees played to build their endurance. One rugged sport Alec played was water polo, and he long remembered a match his unit played against a team from St. Mary's Medical School in London. However, the British Army had so many volunteers that Alec was never sent to South Africa to fight in the Boer War, which the British won in 1902.

A short time before the war ended, an uncle of Alec's died and left him 250 pounds—equal to about $20,000 in today's U.S. money. Thanks to his inheritance, he decided to give up his job at the shipping office and study medicine.

Alec knew nothing about any of the twelve medical schools in London, he later explained. "But I had played water polo against St. Mary's, and so to St. Mary's I went." He couldn't have known it when he enrolled at St. Mary's Medical School in October of 1901, but he would be associated with the institution for half a century.

Alec was a brilliant medical student. Year after year he won prizes and scholarships, and in July of 1906 he passed the tests to become a physician and surgeon.

Treating patients was not his favorite part of medicine, Alec discovered. What he liked best was experimenting. In 1906 he was hired as a researcher at St. Mary's Hospital. He went to work with a team of eight or nine other scientists under the well-known bacteriologist Almoth Wright. Alec worked on various projects involving the prevention and treatment of bacterial infections. One of his specialties was infections caused by wounds. During World War I (1914–1918) he did important research that helped doctors save the lives of many wounded soldiers.

As with his army training, Alec's endurance helped him as a researcher.

Dr. Alexander Fleming

"Little Flem," as his coworkers called him, often remained at his microscope until 2:00 A.M. Yet after a few hours of sleep he would be back in his laboratory, fresh and ready to work, at nine the next morning. When Alec and his colleagues needed blood samples they often drew them from themselves, and when they wanted to try out experimental vaccines, they injected themselves with the preparations.

By temperament Alec was shy and extremely quiet. For recreation, he still loved to make up games, just as he had as a child. He concocted his own version of golf in which he lay flat on the green and used his club like a pool cue to knock the ball toward the hole. On rainy days he played indoor golf and card games of his own invention, or pitched coins at a target. He played his favorite game, billiards, with an artist friend who had lost his hearing during World War I. Since the artist couldn't hear, and Alec preferred not to talk, the two men got along fine. Fleming was an amateur artist, too, with a style all his own. He drew outlines of such subjects as dancing ballerinas, flowers, flags, and mothers with babies, then filled them in with colonies of various bright-colored bacteria. These unusual works of art composed of actual bacteria were called "germ paintings."

In the early 1900s the Fleming brothers became friendly with twin sisters from Ireland. Sarah and Elizabeth McElroy were trained nurses who ran a London nursing home. Sarah was as friendly and talkative as Alec was introverted. According to Fleming family lore, Alec was too shy to propose marriage, so Sarah proposed to him. The couple married in late 1915 when Alec was thirty-four. They moved into their own home, but Alec remained close to his birth family, especially since his older brother John married Sarah's twin, Elizabeth! Alec invented a special game that he and Sarah enjoyed with relatives and friends. They lit up their yard with candles and played "midnight croquet."

Fleming applied his creativity to his research work. During the winter of 1921–1922, he came down with a cold. Not wanting to waste his germs, and curious about what would happen, he took some of his own nasal mucus and placed it on a petri dish on which he was growing bacteria. To his surprise, the microbes didn't grow near the mucus. Apparently something in the mucus prevented the growth of microbes in its vicinity.

He then experimented with tears to see if they, too, could inhibit germ growth. Alec collected his own tears by squeezing lemons near his eyes. Since he couldn't get enough from himself, he paid the laboratory maintenance workers a few pennies each time they allowed him to collect their tears with the lemon treatment. Once, when noticing that a man's eyes were red from crying, Alec told him: "If you cry often enough, you'll be able to retire!"

Alec collected his own tears by squeezing lemons near his eyes.

It turned out that, like mucus, tears contain a substance that can destroy certain microbes. Fleming obtained other samples from patients in the hospital's operating theater and from dead bodies in the postmortem room. He found that saliva, skin, internal organs, and even nails and hair contain a substance that naturally dissolves microbes. Fleming's breakthrough, made in 1921, was his first noteworthy medical discovery. The naturally occurring substance that destroys bacteria was named *lysozyme*—from Greek words roughly meaning "something that has the power to dissolve certain substances." Unfortunately, the microbes lysozyme destroyed proved to be relatively harmless rather than germs that cause serious diseases. Yet his lysozyme work paved the way for Fleming to make a much more momentous discovery seven years later.

By 1928 Alexander Fleming was forty-seven years old. He and Sarah had a four-year-old son, Robert. Alec no longer worked the incredibly long hours he had put in twenty-two years earlier when he was first hired by St. Mary's. It appeared that he would go through life like thousands of other researchers: writing scientific papers and making small breakthroughs that gradually increase human knowledge. Then came the September day in 1928 when, thanks to his habit of observing *everything*, he noticed that a mold had destroyed the staphylococci bacteria.

It appeared that by observing how the mold affected a plateful of bacteria, Alexander Fleming had discovered a miracle drug.

That first day he showed the petri dish with the mold on it to everyone who entered his laboratory. "Take a look at that," he said to one colleague. "It's interesting—the kind of thing I like. It may well turn out to be important."

Identifying the remarkable mold was crucial. Since Fleming knew little about the subject, he read books about molds. He determined that it was of the *Penicillium* group, but which *Penicillium* he didn't know. Later an American mycologist (an expert on molds and other fungi) figured out from a sample that the mold was *Penicillium notatum*. It had probably blown in through the open window or door of Fleming's laboratory and landed on the petri dish.

Alec began experimenting with samples of the mold. His excitement grew as he learned that it had the ability to attack germs that caused many diseases, including strep throat, scarlet fever, pneumonia, blood poisoning, meningitis, diphtheria, and rheumatic fever. It appeared that by observing how the mold affected a plateful of bacteria, Alexander Fleming had discovered a miracle drug. When talking about it, Fleming referred to the antibacterial substance he had discovered as "mold juice," but he knew he needed a more scientific-sounding name. Since the substance came from a *Penicillium* mold, he named it *penicillin*.

But several things had to happen before penicillin could become a successful medication. For one, it had to be tested. He injected his "mold juice" into mice and rabbits and found that it was not harmful. Then he looked for opportunities to try penicillin on human subjects.

St. Mary's Hospital had a patient whose leg was amputated after she fell under a bus. The woman had developed blood poisoning and appeared certain to die. Fleming soaked a dressing in his mold juice and applied it to the infected area. But applying the penicillin directly to the wound wasn't the best way to treat the patient, and besides, the dosage Fleming prepared was relatively weak. The woman died as expected.

Two other tests were more successful. An assistant of Fleming's, Dr. Stuart Craddock, was suffering from an infected nasal passage. On January 9, 1929, Fleming applied penicillin to Craddock's infected nose. The

The big round object on the petri dish is a Penicillium *mold.*

treatment worked pretty well, killing much of the infection. Another colleague, Dr. K. B. Rogers, had an eye infection called conjunctivitis. Fleming applied penicillin to his eye, and the infection quickly disappeared.

But Alexander Fleming couldn't overcome every obstacle. Obtaining medicines from living things was similar to prospecting for gold. The precious metal had to be separated from unwanted material, such as rock, gravel, and sand. Likewise, the antibacterial portion of the *Penicillium* mold had to be extracted from the unwanted parts to make an effective medicine. This is known as purifying the drug. Also, a method of producing penicillin in large amounts had to be developed.

Fleming, who was not a chemist, wasn't prepared to tackle these problems. He asked two colleagues, Dr. Stuart Craddock (whose nose had been treated with penicillin) and Dr. Frederick Ridley, to attempt this crucial part of the work. The two young men, who had only recently completed their medical studies, conducted their penicillin experiments on tables set up in a corridor. Using large bottles containing broth, Craddock and Ridley grew so much *Penicillium* that their colleagues complained about the musty smell in the corridor. By treating the mold with chemicals, they came fairly close, but in the end they failed to extract pure penicillin.

Another possible path to success was open to Fleming. Scientists are expected to write about their discoveries, as Dr. Crawford Long had learned the hard way about anesthesia. Among other things, describing a discovery in print enables other scientists to verify the results and perhaps make further advances. If Fleming could interest the scientific world in penicillin, other researchers might work on the problem of purifying the drug.

Fleming wrote a paper on penicillin. On February 13, 1929, he read it to the Medical Research Club, which Almoth Wright, his boss at St. Mary's, had helped to start nearly fifty years earlier. Fleming's poor communication skills hurt his cause. He was so nervous, and spoke so quietly, that the audience could barely hear him. "He was very shy, and modest in his presentation," the Medical Research Club's chairman later recalled. "He gave it in a halfhearted sort of way, shrugging his shoulders as though he were deprecating the importance of what he said."

It was traditional for Medical Research Club members to show that a particular presentation interested them by asking numerous questions afterward. Not a single question was asked after Fleming finished reading his paper. The audience came away thinking that penicillin was of minor importance, like lysozyme.

Fleming's poor communication skills hurt his cause. He was so nervous, and spoke so quietly, that the audience could barely hear him.

He then wrote another paper, "On the Antibacterial Action of Cultures of a *Penicillium*," which the *British Journal of Experimental Pathology* published in June 1929. Near the end of this paper he declared that penicillin "may be an efficient antiseptic for application to, or injection into, areas infected with penicillin-sensitive microbes." But few scientists who read the article grasped the importance of Fleming's discovery.

Over the next few years, Alexander Fleming worked on a number of projects, including more penicillin experiments and articles. Still, the problem of purifying penicillin remained unsolved.

Meanwhile, two researchers at England's Oxford University became interested in penicillin. One was Howard Florey, who was born in Australia. The other was Ernst Chain, a German-born Jewish scientist who fled Nazi persecution in his native country. In the late 1930s Florey and Chain led a scientific team that worked on purifying penicillin with the idea that it could be injected into the body.

World War II was just beginning. Since penicillin could be a tremendous boon to wounded and sick soldiers, Florey and Chain were provided with money, assistants, and fine laboratory equipment. By 1940 the Florey-Chain team had devised chemical techniques for purifying penicillin and producing it in large quantities. On May 25 of that year the Oxford penicillin team made a historic test. Eight mice were injected with a deadly dose of dangerous germs. Four of the mice were also injected with penicillin, while the other four were left untreated. Within a day all four untreated mice died, while the four that received penicillin shots were in good health. The team quickly repeated the experiment, with the same results.

The Oxford team then tried penicillin on dangerously ill patients. A policeman with a massive infection was saved by penicillin (although he later died when treatment was stopped). A fifteen-year-old boy who had developed a terrible infection following hip surgery recovered completely,

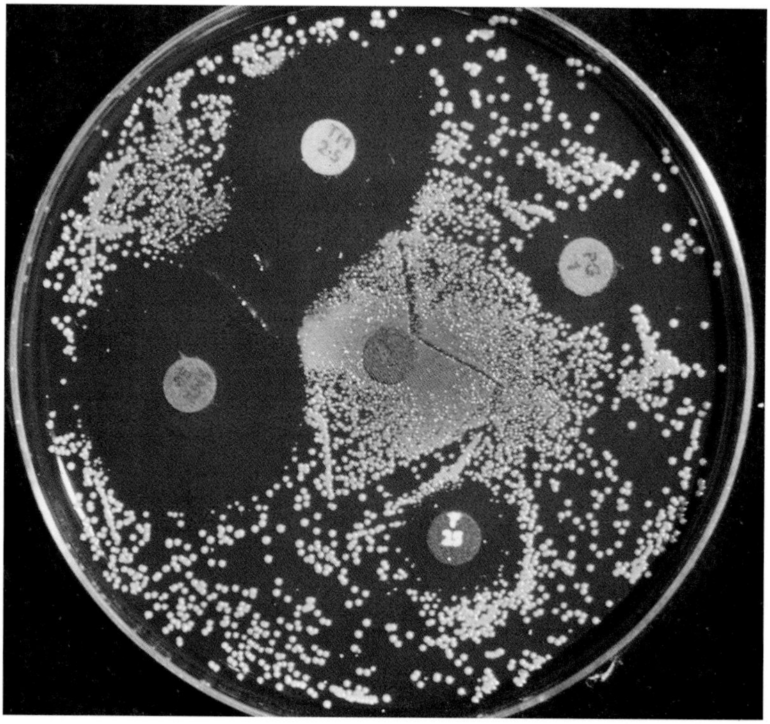

The five round spots on the plate are different antibiotics, and the many small objects are staphylococci bacteria; the experiment shows that some antibiotics have more power than others to kill the germs.

thanks to penicillin treatments. From these and other tests, the Oxford team became convinced that they had developed a major new lifesaving drug.

With the help of an American research laboratory in Peoria, Illinois, huge amounts of penicillin were produced. Penicillin ushered in a new era of antibiotics—powerful drugs obtained from various organisms. Later, other antibiotics were developed. The drugs are taken in the form of pills, introduced intravenously, injected as "shots," and in certain cases applied as ointments. Penicillin and other antibiotics have saved countless lives around the world. In the United States alone, millions of people are alive today only because they were saved by antibiotics.

"Never neglect an extraordinary appearance or happening."

The 1945 Nobel Prize in medicine was awarded to the scientists who had done the most to give penicillin to the world: Alexander Fleming for discovering it, and Howard Florey and Ernst Chain for developing it as an antibiotic medicine. The three men had needed one another to make their mark in science. Florey and Chain couldn't have developed penicillin as a medicine if Fleming hadn't discovered it. And Fleming gained immense fame as its discoverer only after the other two men succeeded in developing penicillin.

Dr. Fleming, who became known as the Penicillin Man, traveled around the world, receiving awards and making speeches. He often pointed out that while good luck accounted for the mold landing on his laboratory dish, he was observant enough to take advantage of the opportunity.

"If I might offer advice to the young [scientist], it would be this," Fleming once said. "Never neglect an extraordinary appearance or happening. It may be a false alarm which leads to nothing, but it may on the other hand be the clue to lead you to some important advance."

Alexander Fleming died in 1955 at the age of seventy-three. Among his papers, a letter was found that he had especially cherished. One of his childhood teachers sent the letter to him about the time that he received the Nobel Prize:

> *Dear little Alex,*
> *Please forgive me—but you were about 8 or 9 years of age at most when I knew you, a dear little boy with dreamy blue eyes. This little letter is just to congratulate my dear little friend of many moons ago and to tell him that I have been following his career and rejoicing in all his wonderful successes. I just have been reading the marvellous story of Penicillin. By the way, your wonderful injections cured a little grand-niece of mine.*

Clyde Tombaugh viii

The Search for Planet X

On a clear, dark night in the year 1918, a twelve-year-old Illinois farm boy named Clyde Tombaugh gazes at the heavens through a small telescope. First he observes our Earth's natural satellite, the moon, with its craters and mountains. Next he aims the instrument, which has a magnifying power of 36, at a brilliant white object. Because he has read a great deal about astronomy, he knows that this body, which is perpetually blanketed in clouds, is the planet Venus. Over the next few hours he gazes at the red planet, Mars, with its polar cap and greenish markings, the ringed planet Saturn, which is so exquisite it almost seems unreal, and the giant planet, Jupiter, with its colorful cloud bands and attendant moons. As he studies the heavenly bodies one by one, little does Clyde realize that in just twelve years he will discover a new planet.

Ancient people observed five naked-eye objects in the night sky that resemble stars, but are different in some ways. For one thing, stars twinkle, while these special objects shine steadily. For another, stars remain in the same relative positions over long periods of time, which is why the imaginary star pictures called constellations hardly change over centuries. The five objects that shine with a steady light, on the other hand, do not remain in fixed positions but travel through the constellations from month to month and year to year. The ancient Greeks called the five bright objects that travel through the constellations *planetae*, meaning "wanderers." That word lives on in our name for these objects: *planets*.

For thousands of years, people believed that there were five planets—Mercury, Venus, Mars, Jupiter, and Saturn—and that they all orbited our Earth.

The ancient Romans originated the names that are still applied to the five naked-eye planets. They named the speedy orange planet that stays close to the sun Mercury, for their fleet messenger of the gods. The white planet that is brighter than every other heavenly body except the sun and the moon they named Venus, for their goddess of love and beauty. The blood-red planet reminded the Romans of war, so they called it Mars, for their war god. The yellow planet that moved majestically through the constellations was named Jupiter, for the king of the Roman gods. The golden-colored planet that traveled even more slowly than Jupiter was named Saturn, for the father of the king of the gods.

For thousands of years, people believed that there were five planets—Mercury, Venus, Mars, Jupiter, and Saturn—and that they all orbited our Earth. Then in the 1500s Nicolaus Copernicus showed that the world we live on is also a planet, and that it and the other planets all orbit the sun. When Isaac Newton removed the last doubts about the Copernican System by the year 1700, educated people accepted the fact that our Earth was a planet, too. If we could go back to the early 1700s and ask young Benjamin Franklin how many planets orbited the sun, he would say six: Mercury, Venus, Earth, Mars, Jupiter, and Saturn.

By then astronomers had a valuable new tool. The Dutch spectacle-maker Hans Lippershey is credited with building the first telescope in 1608, when he placed two lenses at opposite ends of a tube. By making distant objects appear closer, telescopes were extremely helpful to astronomers. As far back as the 1600s, astronomers used telescopes to search for planets beyond Saturn. There were two ways they might recognize a planet.

Stars are so far away that they remain points of light even through telescopes. On the other hand, planets, being much closer, are ball shaped when seen telescopically. Even in small telescopes Mercury, Venus, Mars, and Jupiter look like miniature balls, while Saturn resembles a ball with handles, because of its rings. If an astronomer spotted a ball-shaped object that wasn't any of the other known planets, it might very well be planet number seven.

The other way to find a new planet was by its motion. The planets are practically next door to us compared to the stars. Saturn, for example, is roughly a billion (1,000,000,000) miles from us. By comparison, the nearest star beyond the sun, Proxima Centauri, is 4.3 light-years or 25 trillion (25,000,000,000,000) miles away. That makes Proxima Centauri's location 25,000 times the distance of Saturn, and other stars are hundreds or even thousands of times farther away. Their relative closeness to us is why the planets can be seen moving, while the stars are so far away that the constellations don't seem to change generation after generation. If an astronomer charted an object wandering through the background stars night after night, it might be a planet.

In March of 1781, William Herschel, a German-born astronomer living in Bath, England, was viewing the sky with his telescope. At the time he was in the midst of a star survey and had little interest in the solar system, which refers to the sun and all objects that orbit it, including the planets and the comets. Suddenly Herschel noticed an odd greenish object in the region of the constellation Gemini the Twins. At first he suspected it to be a comet and even wrote a paper entitled "Account of a Comet," which he sent to the Royal Society of London.

Thanks to William Herschel's written account, other astronomers located the object and determined that it was actually a planet about twice Saturn's distance from the sun. Because Herschel had alerted astronomers to its existence, he was hailed as the discoverer of the seventh planet, which was named Uranus for the Greek and Roman god of the sky. Herschel's discovery was a classic case of serendipity, for he hadn't been looking for a planet at all when he came upon Uranus.

Luck had nothing to do with the discovery of the next planet. Soon after William Herschel discovered it in 1781, Uranus was found to deviate from the orbit it should follow according to Isaac Newton's laws of gravitation and motion. Most astronomers concluded that Uranus varied from its predicted position due to the gravitational pull of a planet still farther away from the sun. By September of 1845, Englishman John Couch Adams, using complex mathematics, had calculated the eighth planet's expected position. The twenty-six-year-old mathematician and astronomer was so accurate that he could have discovered the planet rather easily—*if* he had access to a telescope. He didn't. He also ran into bad luck when he tried to convince other astronomers to point their telescopes where he wanted. For example, Adams's calculations were passed on to William Lassell, an astronomer in Liverpool, England, who had a large telescope. Unfortunately, Lassell was in bed nursing a badly injured ankle and was unable to conduct a planet hunt.

While Adams was doing his calculations, the French scientist Urbain Leverrier was doing the same thing. Leverrier's results were close to those of Adams. Leverrier didn't present his results to other scientists until June of 1846—nearly a year later than Adams—but he had better success at convincing astronomers to search for the planet. On September 23, 1846, Johann Galle and Heinrich d'Arrest of Germany's Berlin Observatory aimed their telescope at the place in the sky recommended by Leverrier. They had been searching for less than an hour when they found a greenish blue planet, which was named Neptune for the Roman god of the sea.

To this day, people argue over who discovered Neptune, much like the anesthesia controversy. Some say it was John Couch Adams, who first predicted the eighth planet's true position. Others insist it was Urbain Leverrier, who, despite presenting his findings later, convinced astronomers to look for the planet. Still others favor Johann Galle and Heinrich d'Arrest, who located the planet in the sky. Complicating matters was the fact that three rival countries—England, France, and Germany—were involved. Even today, books in different countries list different discoverers of Neptune. Generally, however, the credit is split between John Couch Adams and Urbain Leverrier, who both discovered the eighth planet on paper.

Soon after the discovery of Neptune in 1846, astronomers began to think about a ninth planet.

Soon after the discovery of Neptune in 1846, astronomers began to think about a ninth planet. Neither Uranus nor Neptune seemed to orbit the sun precisely as expected. Some object besides Neptune seemed to be tugging at Uranus. Neptune, too, appeared to be pulled at by an unseen object. Several astronomers began searching for a "trans-Neptunian planet," meaning a planet beyond Neptune, in the late 1800s. But by the start of the twentieth century, the planet had not been found.

Astronomer Percival Lowell entered the hunt for the ninth planet in 1905. Lowell first became famous for his studies of Mars. In 1894 he built Lowell Observatory in Flagstaff, Arizona, for the purpose of studying the Red Planet. While observing Mars, Lowell saw what he believed to be canals. He formulated a theory that twenty-foot-tall intelligent beings inhabited Mars. Because their planet was so dry, he claimed, the Martians dug a network of canals through which they pumped water to their crops and cities.

While Lowell's books and lectures were a hit with the public, many astronomers insisted that his imagination was running wild and that the canals were illusions. Hurt that he and his observatory weren't taken seriously by other astronomers, Lowell turned to a subject that involved difficult mathematical calculations and plenty of hard work: the hunt for Planet X, as he called the supposed trans-Neptunian planet. Discovering it was certain to win the respect Percival Lowell craved from his colleagues.

While observing Mars, Lowell saw what he believed to be canals. He formulated a theory that twenty-foot-tall intelligent beings inhabited Mars.

Lowell searched for the ninth planet without success on and off between 1905 and his death in 1916. In the years that followed, the evidence grew that the "canals" had been illusions and that there were no Martians. Lowell's books were pulled off shelves because they were more science fiction than science. To resurrect its reputation and that of its founder, Lowell Observatory began a new hunt for Planet X in 1929. Since the observatory couldn't afford to pay an established astronomer to make the search, a young amateur named Clyde Tombaugh was hired to do it.

The oldest of six children, Clyde William Tombaugh was born on a farm near Streator, Illinois, on February 4, 1906. His family grew corn and wheat. When I visited Clyde at his New Mexico home three months before his ninetieth birthday, he explained what it was like growing up on a farm in the early 1900s:

"In those days we didn't have labor-saving machinery. You either worked hard or you didn't survive," he said. Clyde, who was fascinated by numbers, once figured that he husked 7,000 bushels of corn over several years. Since a bushel of corn weighs about 56 pounds, that amounted to roughly 400,000 pounds of husked corn.

Clyde attended a two-room schoolhouse, where his favorite subjects were geography and history. In sixth grade, it suddenly occurred to him that he knew a great deal about Earth's geography but little about the landscape on Mars and the other planets. He went to the Streator Library and began taking out astronomy books.

"I read about William Herschel, who became one of my heroes," Tombaugh told me. "He was a persistent astronomer. He discovered Uranus, made surveys of the sky, and helped us understand the Milky Way. I also read about Adams and Leverrier when I was about twelve years old, and a year or two later I read about Percival Lowell."

At the age of twelve Clyde looked through a small telescope that his uncle owned. Although its magnifying power was only 36 (meaning that it made objects look thirty-six times as big as they appeared to the naked eye), it provided marvelous views of the moon and planets. Clyde was immediately hooked on astronomy. When he was sixteen, his family moved to a farm near Burdett, Kansas. The high-school student devoted his evenings to astronomy. On cloudy nights, he read astronomy books by the light of a kerosene lamp. When it was clear, he observed with a small telescope, while yearning for a more powerful instrument.

"I couldn't afford to buy larger telescopes, so I began to make them," he recalled. In 1928 he completed a nine-inch-diameter reflecting telescope—quite a large instrument for a twenty-two-year-old amateur to build.

His family couldn't afford to send Clyde to college. What would he become? He had experienced too many hard times on the farm to grow

Clyde Tombaugh at the age of twenty-two with the nine-inch-diameter reflecting telescope he completed in 1928.

crops for a living. He thought of becoming a railroad engineer, or setting up a little business of making and selling telescopes. Meanwhile, in late 1928 he sent several drawings he had made of Mars and Jupiter to Lowell Observatory, in the hope of receiving some encouragement or advice. Following an exchange of letters, Dr. Vesto Slipher, the Lowell Observatory director, made Clyde an offer: "Would you be interested in coming to Flagstaff on a few months' trial basis, about the middle of January?"

Clyde didn't know what kind of job he would be doing, but the prospect of working at a large observatory thrilled him. On a January day in 1929 he said good-bye to his family, boarded a train, and made a twenty-eight-hour trip to Flagstaff, Arizona, where Dr. Slipher met him at the depot.

Clyde was to continue Percival Lowell's hunt for Planet X, Slipher explained the next day. The planets are located in the Zodiac, a belt of twelve constellations stretching across the sky. Clyde was to photograph part of the Zodiac each night, including both the region where Lowell had believed Planet X would be found as well as other places along the belt. After taking each picture, he was to photograph the same exact region of the sky several nights later.

The two photographs would be placed in the observatory's Blink-Microscope-Comparator. This is an instrument that magnifies astrophotographs (astronomical photographs) and enables the observer to quickly compare two photos of the same region of the sky. As the observer looks through the eyepiece, the Comparator provides alternating views of first one photograph and then the other. If only stars are on the two photographic plates, the two pictures will appear identical. But if a planet has been captured on the photographs, it will appear to move back and forth, wandering among the stars, as the two plates blink on and off.

Clyde Tombaugh began photographing the sky on April 6, 1929.

Following a thirteen-year interruption, Lowell Observatory's planetary hunt had resumed. Clyde thought that while he would be the photographer, a veteran astronomer would look for the planet on the Comparator. This was the tricky part, for even a momentary lapse in concentration could result in the planet being missed by the viewer. But the veteran astronomers didn't seem to be interested in blinking the plates. In June of 1929, Dr. Slipher added to Clyde's responsibilities. Besides taking the nightly photographs, he was to do the blinking with the Comparator.

When I visited Clyde Tombaugh in New Mexico in late 1995, one of his old photographs was displayed on his dining room table. The photograph contained so many stars it looked like someone had dumped a pailful of sand on it. There were close to a *million* stars on the photograph, Clyde explained. Since it had been impossible to study all of them at once, he

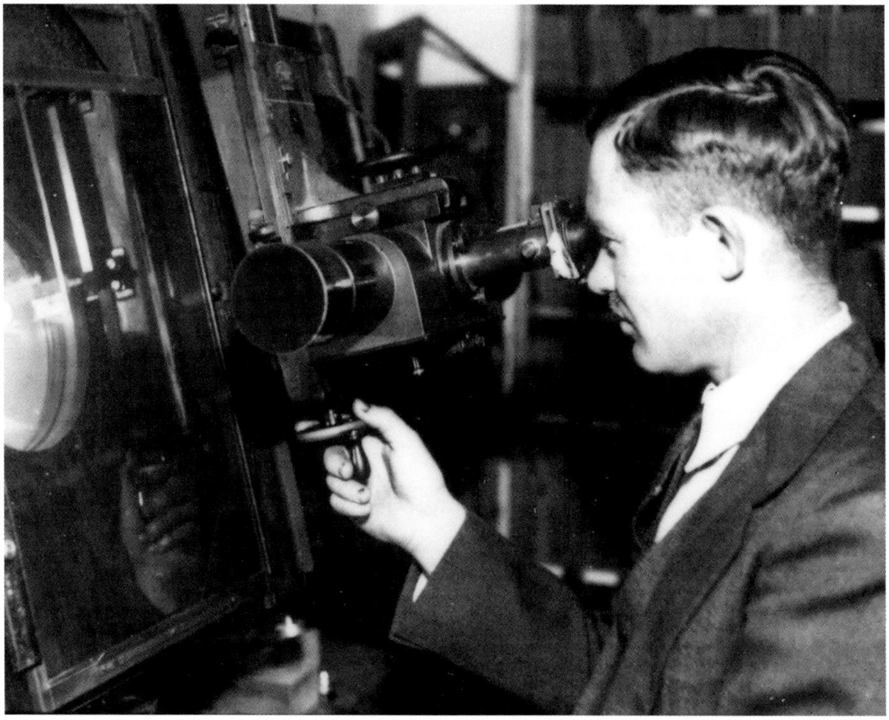

Clyde "blinked" photographs at Lowell Observatory in his search for the ninth planet.

had divided the plates into sections of several hundred stars for viewing on the Comparator.

Clyde realized why the Lowell Observatory staff was having him conduct the entire project. "They had given up," he explained. Even if a ninth planet was out there, they felt it would be like finding a needle in a haystack, so while they *hoped* their observatory would find it, they didn't want to waste a veteran astronomer's time on the project.

"I wasn't terribly optimistic myself," Clyde recalled. "But my attitude was, I'll go through the whole Zodiac thoroughly and systematically, and if I find nothing, then the ninth planet is not there."

"[M]y attitude was, I'll go through the whole Zodiac thoroughly and systematically, and if I find nothing, then the ninth planet is not there."

Week after week, he photographed the sky and blinked the plates, with no sign of Planet X. At about 4:00 P.M. on Tuesday, February 18, 1930, Clyde was blinking two photographs he took in January of the region around Delta Gemini, a star called Delta Gem for short. Suddenly he noticed a dim object that moved slightly among the stars during the six days between photographs.

"That's it!" he said to himself.

Clyde hurried down the hall to Vesto Slipher's office and said: "Dr. Slipher, I have found your Planet X!"

During the next few nights, the Lowell Observatory staff observed and photographed the dim yellowish object. It was indeed the ninth planet. But the observatory wanted to make sure that Percival Lowell, not Clyde Tombaugh, received the glory. Not until March 13, 1930—the seventy-fifth anniversary of Lowell's birth and the 149th anniversary of Herschel's discovery of Uranus—did the observatory issue a statement about the new planet. It gave the credit to Percival Lowell because he had predicted the planet's existence, yet barely mentioned "Mr. C. W. Tombaugh, assistant on the staff." The planet was soon named Pluto, for the Greek and Roman god of the dead. An eleven-year-old English girl, Venetia Burney, proposed this name, which was chosen by the Lowell Observatory staff out of hundreds of suggestions. Early newspaper articles reported that Pluto might be the biggest of the nine planets, larger even than Jupiter.

Clyde was proud of his role in the discovery, but some of his colleagues were jealous of *any* attention he received. Over the next thirteen years (with time out for college) Clyde continued the search for more planets

January 23, 1930

The photographic plates on which Clyde Tombaugh discovered Pluto;

at Lowell Observatory. He didn't find any. Dr. Vesto Slipher, who was resentful that Clyde received more and more credit for the discovery as time passed, abruptly fired him in 1944. Later Clyde Tombaugh became a professor at New Mexico State University, where he helped found its astronomy department.

Meanwhile, bits and pieces of information were being learned about Pluto. Instead of being the largest planet, Pluto proved to be the smallest. Pluto wasn't big enough to cause the variations in Uranus's and Neptune's orbits that led astronomers to look for another planet in the first place!

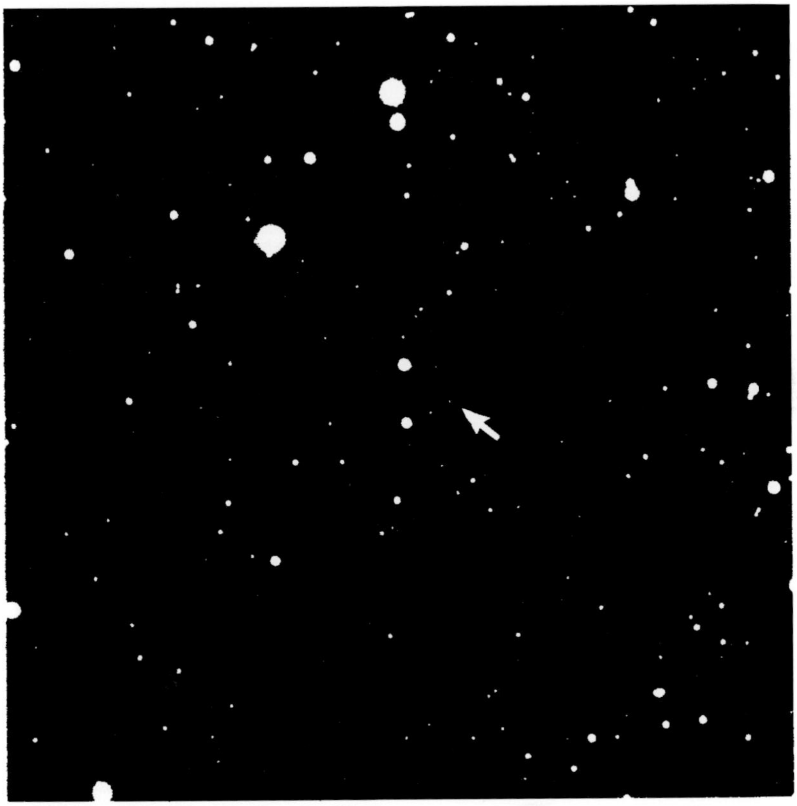

January 29, 1930

the ninth planet is the dim object (pointed out by the arrows) that moved slightly among the stars over a few days.

What's more, those variations didn't even exist, as revealed by the *Voyager 2* space probe that approached Uranus in 1986 and Neptune in 1989.

"The discovery of Pluto was due to a remarkable chain of accidental events spanning several decades," Clyde Tombaugh wrote in his book, *Out of the Darkness*. One of those fortunate mistakes was the astronomers' erroneous idea about quirks in the orbits of Uranus and Neptune. Another

Venetia Burney, the eleven-year-old English girl who named Pluto.

was Percival Lowell's weird notions about Mars, which inspired him to begin the search for the ninth planet.

By the 1950s, when I was growing up, astronomers had adopted the attitude that prevails today. Clyde Tombaugh discovered the ninth planet through his thorough and systematic photography and examination of photographic plates. But Percival Lowell must receive some credit for beginning the search.

On a personal note, after I read about Clyde Tombaugh as a child, he became my astronomical hero, so I was nervous when I went to interview him in 1995. As I rang the doorbell of his home near Las Cruces, New Mexico, I thought: I'm about to meet *Clyde Tombaugh*! He turned out to be the nicest and funniest man this side of Pluto. Pointing to the horse farm nearby, he said: "I like living close to horses because they make good *neighhhh*-bors!" Later Clyde quipped, "Pluto is a good name for the planet because it was so doggone hard to find," referring to the cartoon dog who made his screen debut a few months after the discovery of the ninth planet. How could anyone be nervous after hearing jokes like that? Clyde Tombaugh died in 1997, shortly before what would have been his ninety-first birthday.

Most astronomers were convinced that Pluto was the final planet that would ever be found in the solar system. Then in 2005 astronomers observing distant realms of the solar system detected a tenth planet. The newest member of the sun's planetary family is about nine billion miles from the sun—more than twice Pluto's distance—and appears to be a little larger than Pluto. This, too, was a serendipitous discovery, for the astronomers who located it did not expect to find a planet in the outer regions of the solar system they were studying.

ix Lise Meitner

The Discovery of Nuclear Fission

As a young child, Lise Meitner performed an experiment that she feared would end the world.

Like most girls of the 1800s, Lise learned to sew at an early age. But she was told by her grandmother that if she sewed on the Sabbath (Saturday for Jewish people), the heavens would come crashing down on Earth. One Saturday Lise decided to test her grandmother's warning. She did a stitch of her embroidery, then went to the window and looked at the sky. It was still up where it belonged. She did another stitch, then another, and still the sky did not fall. Lise learned to test things for herself rather than believe everything she was told. Yet in a strange way her grandmother was right, for many years later Lise's work would result in a device that *could* end the world—or at least mankind's existence in it.

The third of eight children, Lise Meitner was born into a Jewish family in Vienna, Austria, in November of 1878, thirteen years after Ignaz

Semmelweis died in that city. Her mother was a gifted pianist who taught Lise and her other children music. Lise's father was a successful lawyer.

Lise first became intrigued by science as a child when she noticed an oil slick in a puddle of water. Wondering what created the pretty colors, she decided that one day she would understand the secrets of nature. The Meitner house had plenty of books. It was said that by age eight Lise loved to read so much that she slept with mathematics and science books under her pillow.

Lise attended a school near her home. She was a fine student, but that didn't matter. As in many other countries at that time, Austria permitted only boys to attend the high schools that prepared students for a university education. Public schooling for girls ended at age fourteen. A few months before her fourteenth birthday Lise received a report card with the words

Vienna, Austria, in the 1870s at about the time Lise Meitner was born there.

vom weiteren Schulbesuch befreit written on it. This was German (the language spoken in Austria), meaning "released from further schooling." Lise was expected to help her mother at home for a few years and then get married, but she had other plans.

During the 1890s some exciting discoveries were made by physicists—scientists who study matter and energy. In 1895, the year Lise turned seventeen, the German physicist Wilhelm Roentgen discovered X-rays, a kind of radiation that can show the inside of the human body. The next year Antoine Henri Becquerel, a French physicist, discovered that uranium is radioactive, meaning that it emits high-energy atomic particles and rays. Lise informed her parents that she wanted to become a physicist, like Roentgen, Becquerel, or the Polish-born Marie Curie, one of the few women in the field.

With the college preparatory schools closed to girls, Lise would have to be privately tutored to have any chance of attending a university.

With the college preparatory schools closed to girls, Lise would have to be privately tutored to have any chance of attending a university. But her parents were concerned about her future. She showed no interest in marriage. If she couldn't become a physicist, how would she earn a living? They offered her a deal. First, she must earn a teaching certificate so that she would have a dependable means of support. Then, if she still wanted to study physics at a university, they would hire tutors to prepare her.

At eighteen, Lise began studying to become a French teacher. Upon earning her teaching certificate three years later, in 1899, she still wanted to become a physicist. Her parents kept their promise and arranged for Lise to study with private tutors. Meanwhile, the government decided that females who passed the same test administered to male students could attend Austrian universities. This meant that if her tutors could prepare her to pass the test, Lise might attend the great University of Vienna in her home city.

Starting in 1899, Lise studied Greek, Latin, history, religion, mathematics, and physics and other sciences with tutors. She studied day and night, packing about eight years of work into two. Her brothers and sisters became so accustomed to seeing her with a book in her hands that whenever she was without one they teased, "Lise, you're going to flunk!"

In July of 1901, at a school on Beethovenplatz (Beethoven Place), Lise took the examination she had been preparing for. Sixty-three years later, Lise Meitner recalled how frightened she had been to take this test in unfamiliar surroundings. In her article "Looking Back" in the November 1964 *Bulletin of the Atomic Scientists*, eighty-six-year-old Meitner wrote: "We were fourteen girls in all and took a not altogether easy exam (only four of us got through) at a boys' school in Vienna."

Lise Meitner in about 1900 at approximately twenty-two years of age.

Lise was one of the four young women who passed, and in October of 1901 she enrolled at the University of Vienna. She was about to turn twenty-three—rather old to be starting college. Eager to make up for lost time, she signed up for an extremely heavy class load. "From 1901 until the end of 1905, I studied mathematics, physics, and philosophy at Vienna University," she related in her "Looking Back" article. "No doubt, like many other young students, I began by attending too many lectures. Indeed, at that time it was very unusual for a girl to attend university lectures at all."

Her second year at the university, she began an intensive series of physics courses. Her favorite professor, famed physicist Ludwig Boltzmann, had a love for the subject that Lise found infectious. "Boltzmann had no inhibitions whatever about showing his enthusiasm while he spoke," Lise recalled in 1964, "and this naturally carried his listeners along." Lise especially enjoyed hearing Professor Boltzmann talk about the opposition he encountered a few years earlier, when he had been one of the first scientists to believe in the existence of atoms. At a time when other professors resented having females in their classes, Boltzmann recognized Lise's brilliance and encouraged her to dedicate her life to physics.

Lise Meitner completed her basic coursework in mid-1905, then remained at the university for her doctoral degree, which she received on February 1, 1906. She was only the second woman to be awarded a physics doctorate by the University of Vienna. The small, slender young woman with intense eyes was now *Dr.* Meitner, but Lise had a problem. She couldn't find a paying job in physics either at a university or in industry. She wrote a letter to Marie Curie in Paris, hoping to be hired as an assistant in her laboratory. But Marie Curie, who shared the 1903 Nobel Prize for Physics with her husband, Pierre Curie, and Antoine Henri Becquerel for their studies of uranium and radioactivity, had no position to offer Lise.

Dr. Meitner found that her teaching certificate came in handy. For about a year she spent her days teaching in a girls' school. At night, she worked as a volunteer in the University of Vienna physics laboratory. In 1898 Marie and Pierre Curie had discovered the radioactive chemical elements radium and polonium, and by the early 1900s radioactivity was a popular topic among physicists. Lise began writing papers about radioactivity, but she had no inkling that it would become her life's work.

Germany, the birthplace of such great physicists as Albert Einstein and Max Planck, was the leading center for science in the early 1900s. In 1907 Lise Meitner, now approaching her twenty-ninth birthday, decided to visit Germany for additional study. That September she arrived in Berlin, where she expected to attend Planck's lectures at the University of Berlin for a year or so. As it turned out, she would remain in Germany for more than thirty years.

Otto Hahn, Lise Meitner (center), and either Emma or Grete Planck. Physicist Max Planck had identical twin daughters, one of whom would be in a photograph while the other took it.

While attending Planck's lectures, Lise met Otto Hahn, a chemist her age who shared her scientific interests. Hahn, who worked at Berlin's Chemistry Institute, was looking for a physicist to help with his research on radioactivity and asked Lise if she wanted the job. Unfortunately, the head of the Institute, Nobel Prize–winning chemist Emil Fischer, was biased against women scientists. Lise could work at his Institute, Fischer said, but only under certain conditions. She must never enter any part of the Institute building used by the men. Instead, she must set up her laboratory in what had been the basement carpentry shop. Furthermore, she couldn't enter the Institute's bathrooms, but must go down the street to a ladies' room in a restaurant.

Colleagues who saw her walking with Hahn along the streets would often say "Good day, Herr Hahn" while ignoring her as if she didn't exist.

Lise needed a job, so she accepted these conditions and went to work in her basement laboratory. After about a year, the restrictions were lifted. Meitner gained access to the entire building, and a ladies' room was installed, yet she still encountered prejudice from many of the male scientists. She recalled in "Looking Back" that colleagues who saw her walking with Hahn along the streets would often say "Good day, Herr Hahn" while ignoring her as if she didn't exist.

Lise Meitner had to endure many hardships. At first she wasn't paid at all but depended on a small allowance her family provided. Later she received a salary so small that she sometimes had nothing but coffee and black bread for food. Along with millions of other people, her life was changed by World War I (1914–1918), which pitted the Central Powers, including Austria and Germany, against the United States, France, England, and the other Allies. Meitner spent two years working as an X-ray nurse in an Austrian army hospital near the war zone.

"I never expected it to be as awful as it actually is," she wrote to a friend.

"These poor [injured soldiers], who at best will be cripples, have the most horrible pains. One can hear their screams and groans as well as see their horrible wounds. . . . I work only with the very badly wounded. . . . It is impossible how much they suffer."

During the war, Meitner arranged her leaves to coincide with those of Hahn, who had been called upon to develop poison gases. The pair continued to study the high-energy rays and particles emitted by radioactive substances, and to search for new elements. Meitner and Hahn made one of their greatest discoveries in 1917. In a highly radioactive mineral called pitchblende, they discovered a new element—one of the basic substances, including oxygen, helium, hydrogen, gold, and uranium, that make up the universe. It was suggested that the new element be named Lisotto, combining the names Lise and Otto. However, two British scientists, Frederick Soddy and John Cranston, independently discovered the same new element, also in 1917. Instead of Lisotto, the element was named protactinium. On lists of the elements, Lise Meitner, Otto Hahn, Frederick Soddy, and John Cranston are all named as its discoverers.

At the end of World War I, Dr. Meitner was named head of the department of radiation physics at Berlin's Kaiser Wilhelm Institute. Then, in 1926, she was made a physics professor at the University of Berlin. The forty-eight-year-old scientist became the first female physics professor in Germany. There was an amusing sidelight to one of her university lectures of the 1920s. She called the lecture "*Die Bedeutung der Radioaktivitat fur kosmische Prozesse,*" which means "The Significance of Radioactivity for Cosmic Processes." Thinking that a woman couldn't lecture on such a scholarly subject, a publisher asked for permission to publish her lecture on "The Significance of Radioactivity for Cosmetic [*kosmetische*] Processes."

The 1930s has been called the "golden age" of nuclear physics. In 1932 the neutron was discovered. By then, physicists had a pretty good idea of how the fundamental units of matter, called atoms, are put together.

Atoms are tiny units of matter that make up everything in the universe—from our own bodies to the largest stars. Atoms aren't nearly large enough to be seen by our eyes alone. In fact, they are so small that millions of them could fit on the pointy end of a pin.

Despite being tiny, atoms are gigantic compared to the even smaller particles they contain. The three main types of subatomic particles in atoms are protons, neutrons, and electrons. Protons and neutrons are located in the nucleus, or central core, of an atom. Electrons are located outside the nucleus, which they orbit billions of times each second.

For ages, people wondered: What is it about gold that makes it gold, and what is it about lead that makes it lead and not gold? Physicists discovered the answer in the early 1900s. The number of protons an atom possesses determines its identity. Gold differs from lead because a gold atom has 79 protons while a lead atom has 82 protons. No matter where it happens to be—whether inside a star or in water—an atom with a single proton is hydrogen. An atom with 92 protons must be uranium, while an atom with 91 protons must be the element Lise Meitner helped discover: protactinium. The number of protons an atom has is known as its atomic number. The atomic numbers of gold, lead, hydrogen, uranium, and protactinium are 79, 82, 1, 92, and 91, respectively.

By the 1930s Lise Meitner was specializing in nuclear physics, as the study of the nuclei of atoms became known. Like other nuclear physicists, she bombarded elements with various particles to see what kind of changes she could bring about in atoms.

In 1934 a scientific team headed by Lise Meitner at the Kaiser Wilhelm Institute began what proved to be one of the most important experiments ever. Also on the team were Otto Hahn and a young German chemist named Fritz Strassmann. They exposed uranium to particles given off by other elements. They expected the uranium atoms to absorb the particles and change into new, man-made atoms with atomic numbers higher than uranium. These elements were referred to as *transuranics*, meaning "beyond uranium." Other physicists in Italy and France were doing similar experiments.

The results startled all the scientists attempting to produce transuranics. The particle bombardment did *not* produce elements with atomic numbers larger than 92. The opposite occurred. They produced elements with atomic numbers smaller than uranium. For example, Meitner's team found that some of the uranium seemed to have changed into barium, which has the atomic number 56. Uranium has 92 protons, while barium has 56. The mystery was: What had happened to the other 36 protons?

If she had remained in Germany, Lise Meitner might have been arrested and sent to a death camp.

Before the mystery could be solved, world events changed the course of Lise Meitner's life, and could have ended it. Led by Adolf Hitler, the Nazis had risen to power in Germany in 1932. Hitler and the Nazis persecuted the country's Jewish people. In 1933 Hitler removed Germany's Jews from government positions. Two years later Hitler stripped them of their citizenship rights. By 1938 Nazi mobs were destroying Jewish businesses and burning synagogues. The next year, on September 1, 1939, World War II began with the German invasion of Poland. The Nazis established concentration camps where they imprisoned and killed millions of Jewish people.

Lise Meitner was forced to fill out a form describing her Jewish ancestry. Her case came to the attention of a powerful Nazi leader, Heinrich Himmler. As head of the German police, including the Nazi secret police known as the Gestapo, Himmler ordered the murders of millions of people during the World War II era. If she had remained in Germany, Lise Meitner might have been arrested and sent to a death camp. Before that could happen, some of her physicist friends decided to smuggle her out of the country.

Back in the 1920s, Lise Meitner had gone on a lecture tour in the Netherlands. There she became close friends with the Dutch physicist Dirk Coster and his wife, Miep. Coster, who codiscovered the element hafnium in 1923, had provided a home for a number of Jewish refugees from Germany from 1933 on.

On Monday, July 11, 1938, Professor Coster came to Berlin to rescue Meitner. She didn't have the proper papers to leave Germany, so her escape would be extremely dangerous. Because of Nazi spies who would turn her in if they knew her intentions to flee, Meitner kept to her regular routine. On Tuesday, July 12, she went to the Kaiser Wilhelm Institute the same as usual.

"So as not to arouse suspicion," Meitner later wrote to a friend, "I spent the last day of my life in Germany in the Institute until eight at night correcting a paper to be published by a young associate. Then I had exactly one and a half hours to pack a few necessary things into two small suitcases."

She spent her last night in Berlin at the home of Otto Hahn and his wife, Edith. The next day a friend drove Lise Meitner to the Berlin station. As arranged, she boarded the train and found Dirk Coster already waiting. The two physicists greeted each other as though they had met by chance.

The train followed a lightly traveled railroad route westward toward the Netherlands. During the journey several passengers were pulled from the train and arrested, and at one point a Nazi military patrol demanded to see Meitner's papers. She sat trembling in fear while the Nazi guards studied her old Austrian passport, which was no longer valid. Fortunately, the guards let the 110-pound, middle-aged woman continue her journey.

On the afternoon of July 13, 1938, the train passed over the border into the Netherlands. After thirty-one years in Germany, fifty-nine-year-old Lise Meitner was beginning a new life.

Lise got away just in time. Kurt Hess, a chemist at the Institute who was known as a Nazi "fanatic," lived in an apartment adjoining hers in the Institute's housing complex. About the time that Dr. Meitner escaped, Hess wrote a note to Nazi authorities warning that she was about to flee. Fortunately, she was out of the country before anything could be done about it.

"I feel so completely lost and helpless," she wrote to Hahn. Little did she know that her greatest discovery was just weeks away.

Coster first took Meitner to Groningen in the Netherlands. From that city Coster sent Otto Hahn a telegram saying that the "baby" had arrived safely. This was a secret way of letting him know that Lise had escaped Germany. Coster became a hero to physicists around the world for helping to save Meitner. The Austrian physicist Wolfgang Pauli told Coster: "You have made yourself as famous for the rescue of Lise Meitner as for the discovery of hafnium."

Lise now had to find a job. Nobel Prize–winning physicist Karl Manne Siegbahn had recently become director of the Nobel Institute for Physics in Stockholm, the capital of Sweden. Dr. Siegbahn asked Lise to work at his institute, which was Sweden's first nuclear research facility. Meitner moved to Stockholm in August of 1938 and went to work at the Nobel Institute for Physics. Meitner soon wrote to Hahn that she felt like a "nonperson, or someone who is buried alive," in Sweden. She arrived in the country with little more than the clothes on her back. She didn't know the language. She lived in a small room in a hotel, and her family was back in Austria. Moreover, Siegbahn didn't provide Meitner with laboratory equipment for experimentation and seemed to view her as a clerk. "I feel so completely lost and helpless," she wrote to Otto Hahn on September 21, 1938, as her sixtieth birthday approached. Little did she know that her greatest discovery was just weeks away.

Otto Hahn and Lise Meitner exchanged letters regularly, discussing various topics in physics. Hahn and Fritz Strassmann continued to bombard uranium with particles from other elements. They still found that barium was produced, and the mystery of the 36 missing protons remained unsolved.

A nephew of Lise's named Otto Frisch was a physicist in Copenhagen, Denmark. In late 1938, Lise and her nephew were invited to spend the holidays with a family who lived along Sweden's western coast. While there, Frisch decided to go cross-country skiing around Christmas Day. His aunt hadn't any skis, but she was a powerful walker and said she would walk beside him as he skied.

As they traveled through the snow, Meitner reviewed the mystery with her nephew. She, Hahn, and Strassmann had attempted to create transuranic elements by bombarding uranium with subatomic particles. But instead of transuranics, they had produced barium.

The two physicists sat down on a fallen tree. They discussed the possibilities and added and subtracted several atomic numbers on scraps of paper. Within an hour they had the solution.

By bombarding the uranium with subatomic particles, Meitner and her team in Berlin hadn't increased the number of protons in the atomic nuclei. Instead, they had accomplished something completely unexpected: They had split the nuclei of the uranium atoms in two, transforming them into two other elements.

One of the elements was barium. Finding what the other must be required only simple arithmetic. Since uranium has 92 and barium 56 protons, the other element could be determined by subtraction:

$$92 - 56 = x$$

The answer, of course, was 36. Meitner knew the elements' atomic numbers by heart. Krypton was the element with atomic number 36. The other element produced must be krypton.

Meitner and Frisch wrote a short paper about the splitting of the uranium atoms that the journal *Nature* published on February 11, 1939. Soon laboratories around the world confirmed that by splitting uranium atoms with subatomic particles, uranium could be converted into two other elements totaling atomic number 92, such as barium and krypton (56+36) or rubidium and cesium (37+55). But there was more to the story than that—*much* more.

Journalists began to call Lise Meitner "the Mother of the Atomic Bomb"—a nickname she detested.

The splitting of the nuclei of uranium atoms released a great deal of energy. In fact, once the nucleus of a uranium atom was split, more particles were released, which could split other uranium nuclei. This began a chain reaction—an event that can release humungous amounts of energy. Lise Meitner and Otto Frisch named the process of splitting atomic nuclei into two parts *fission*, from a Latin word meaning "to split." Lise Meitner, Otto Hahn, Fritz Strassmann, and Otto Frisch all contributed to the discovery of nuclear fission.

Their discovery had an unforeseen result. Scientists soon used the fission process to develop the atomic bomb. In 1943, Lise Meitner was invited to go to Los Alamos, New Mexico, to help create this incredibly powerful weapon. She refused, saying, "I will have nothing to do with bombs!" They were produced nonetheless. On August 6, 1945, the United States dropped an atomic bomb on the city of Hiroshima, Japan. At the point of the explosion the temperature reached ninety million degrees Fahrenheit, which is hotter than the core of the sun. Approximately 100,000 people

The mushroom cloud over Nagasaki, Japan, following the explosion of an atomic bomb on August 9, 1945.

were killed during or soon after the blast. Three days later, the United States dropped another A-bomb on the city of Nagasaki, Japan, killing about 40,000 people. These atomic bomb attacks helped end World War II. Ever since, however, people have debated whether it was acceptable to use such powerful weapons on other human beings, even in wartime.

Journalists began to call Lise Meitner "the Mother of the Atomic Bomb" —a nickname she detested. For the rest of her life, she pointed out that the discovery of fission came serendipitously, when she and her team were trying to produce transuranic elements. In an interview published in the January 5, 1946, *Saturday Evening Post*, Meitner explained:

> *I have not designed any atomic bomb. I don't even know what one looks like, nor how it works technically. I must stress that I*

Lise Meitner with President Harry S. Truman on the occasion of her "Woman of the Year" award from the National Women's Press Club on February 9, 1946.

> *myself have not in any way worked on the smashing of the atom with the idea of producing death-dealing weapons. You must not blame us scientists for the use to which war technicians have put our discoveries.*

But fission wasn't used to produce just "death-dealing weapons." It was also employed for peaceful purposes. Nuclear reactors work by the fission process. These machines split the nuclei of uranium atoms to produce electric power. Today hundreds of nuclear reactors produce electric power in many countries of the world, including the United States.

Lise Meitner won several prizes for her work. Among them was the Enrico Fermi Prize of the U.S. Atomic Energy Commission for her contribution to the discovery of nuclear fission.

Dr. Meitner lived in Sweden for twenty-two years. Then in 1960, at the age of eighty-two, she retired and moved to England to be near her nephew Otto Frisch and his family. In 1967 Lise Meitner fell and broke her hip and also suffered several strokes. On October 27, 1968, shortly before what would have been her ninetieth birthday, Lise Meitner died in her sleep.

Her story wasn't quite finished. In 1982 a group of physicists in West Germany produced a new element with an atomic number of 109. It was named meitnerium to honor Lise Meitner. Peter Armbruster, the leader of the team that made the discovery, explained: "Lise Meitner should be honored for her fundamental work on the physical understanding of fission. She should be honored as the most significant woman scientist of this century."

Muhammad Ahmed el-Hamed

X

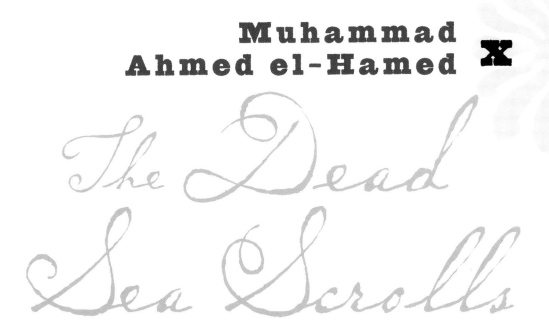

The Dead Sea Scrolls

Nearly two thousand years ago, a group of men wearing white robes climbed along the cliffs near the Dead Sea, about fifteen miles east of what is now Jerusalem, Israel. The men carried what appeared to be ordinary clay jars, but hidden within these vessels were precious treasures. The jars held biblical manuscripts that had been copied over a span of two centuries.

The men were members of a Jewish sect known as the Essenes and lived in a community now known as Khirbat Qumran. Believing that other Jewish people had become too worldly and strayed from the laws of the Bible, the Essenes broke away from their fellow Jews around 150 B.C. They established communities at Khirbat Qumran and at several other nearby locations where they lived simple lives based on worship. Although composed entirely of males, the Essenes managed to keep their sect going by adopting and raising boys who had no parents of their own.

The Essenes, who called themselves the "Children of Light," followed strict rules in their communities. New members had to donate their belongings to the settlement, which shared everything. The members ate, prayed, and studied the Bible together. Everyone in an Essene community had a job. Some men did the cooking or tended the flocks. Others raised bees, which provided honey for food and beeswax for making candles. Still others were artisans who made pottery or clothing. At Khirbat Qumran, men who had fine handwriting copied various parts of the Jewish Old Testament, also known as the Hebrew Bible. The work by these scribes (copiers of manuscripts) was one of the community's main functions. The Essenes believed that the Bible contained God's words and must be preserved for later generations. A piece of pottery with Hebrew letters written on it in a childish handwriting was found centuries later in a rubbish dump at Khirbat Qumran. Apparently the letters were the "homework" of a boy training to become a scribe.

However, in the year A.D. 68, the Essenes' life at Khirbat Qumran was about to come to an end, which was why the men in the white robes were clambering about the cliffs with the clay jars. More than a century earlier, in the year 63 B.C., the Romans seized Judea (an ancient kingdom of the Jews in which the Essenes' communities were located) and made it part of the Roman Empire. Periodically, small groups of Roman soldiers stormed Khirbat Qumran and tortured and murdered some of its inhabitants. Now, having received word that numerous Roman soldiers were headed their way from Jericho, just ten miles away, the Essenes at Khirbat Qumran realized they must flee. Before doing so, the men placed their biblical scrolls in the jars, which they were hiding in cliffside caves. To confuse anyone who might come to destroy the scrolls, they placed some empty jars near those that contained the precious manuscripts.

Once their scrolls were hidden, the men came down from the cliffs. They gathered their belongings and abandoned Khirbat Qumran, never to return. What became of them is a mystery. The Roman soldiers may have killed them, or perhaps they scattered to various locations, like other Jewish people driven by the Romans from Judea.

The Essenes chose fine hiding places. It was said that, more than seven hundred years later, in about the year A.D. 800, an Arab shepherd boy discovered some of the scrolls, but details regarding this are sketchy. In any event, most of the scrolls lay unseen by human eyes and untouched by human hands for nearly nineteen hundred years. When the scrolls were finally discovered, it was partly by luck and partly thanks to the curiosity of a teenage goatherd.

The Essenes chose fine hiding places. Most of the scrolls lay unseen by human eyes and untouched by human hands for nearly nineteen hundred years.

Muhammad Ahmed el-Hamed, a twentieth-century boy, grew up in what was then called Palestine, not far from where the Essenes' community of Khirbat Qumran once stood. Muhammad's people, the Taamirah tribe, were Bedouins. The name *Bedouin* comes from the Arabic word *badawi*, meaning "desert dweller." Traditionally the Bedouins moved about desert regions with their sheep, goats, and camels in search of pastureland, carrying the black tents in which they lived with them.

Little is known about Muhammad's background. He was probably born around 1931 or 1932, but that is not known for certain because Bedouins did not keep records of births or celebrate birthdays. In fact, nearly all authors who have written about him have referred to Muhammad by the wrong name: Muhammad Edh-Dhib or something similar. Dr. John C. Trever, who knew Muhammad and provided the photo of him for this book, told me in 1986 that "Edh-Dhib" is actually a nickname. It means "the Wolf" in Arabic and was given to Muhammad at the time of his birth because his father was said to be "fierce as a wolf." Like other Bedouins,

Muhammad Ahmed el-Hamed with one of his lambs, many years after his discovery of the Dead Sea Scrolls.

Muhammad was a Muslim, meaning that he practiced the religion of Islam.

By the time of Muhammad's childhood his people were no longer completely nomadic. For about half of each year Muhammad lived with his people in a village, called Taamirah, a short way from Bethlehem. In his village he attended a school where he learned to read and write. Muhammad spent the other half of the year—usually from November until May—herding his goats through the countryside between Bethlehem and the Dead Sea. His travels sometimes took him to the spot where the Essenes' Khirbat Qumran community existed long ago.

Each night, when out in what the Bedouins called the Wilderness, the herdsmen counted their animals to make sure none were lost. According to an interview Muhammad gave in Bethlehem in 1956, his great adventure began in 1945, when he was tending a herd of fifty-five goats in the Wilderness along with two men who had herds of their own. It happened that for two nights Muhammad neglected to count his goats, so at about eleven o'clock on the morning of the third day he did a head count. To his dismay, one goat was missing. Muhammad had made a costly blunder, for his people depended on the goats for food and made their black tents out of goat-hair cloth. As he explained in the interview:

> *I went to my companions and told them that I wanted to leave my herd with them and wanted to go out and search for the lost goat. I had to climb hills and go down into valleys. I went very far. As I was roaming, I came upon a cave with its entrance open at the top. Supposing that the goat had fallen into the cave, I started throwing in stones. And every time I threw a stone into the cave, I heard a sound like the breaking of pottery.*

By good fortune, Muhammad had stumbled upon an extremely special cave. Also by luck, the stones he threw happened to hit the jars. Many people would have been hesitant to enter a dark and unknown cave. But Muhammad, who was only about thirteen or fourteen years old according to this version of the story, was very curious about what might be in the cave, so he climbed in through a small opening. Inside the cave he saw a number of pottery jars, which aroused his interest. Continuing his story, he explained what he did next:

> *I began to break the jars with my staff, thinking I would find treasure. However, in the first nine jars which I broke, I found little reddish seeds, and nothing else. When I broke the tenth jar, which was the smallest of the jars, I found in it some rolled leather scrolls with scrawling on them. I wrapped up the leather in my cloak and departed. When I reached my companions, I showed them what I had found. Through my lack of good fortune, I did not find the goat. I kept the leather with me until I returned to our house, where I put it in a skin bag and hung it up in a corner. The skin bag remained hanging there for more than two years. Afterward an uncle of mine came to our house and asked that he might take the scrolls and show them to a dealer in antiquities at Bethlehem, to see if they might be of any value.*

In later interviews, Muhammad Ahmed el-Hamed and his older cousins Jum'a Muhammad Khalil and Khalil Musa told a different version of how the precious scrolls were discovered. This later version was put together through interviews gathered by Dr. John C. Trever, who recounted it in his 1965 book *The Untold Story of Qumran.*

According to this story, Muhammad and his two cousins were tending sheep and goats along the hills of Khirbat Qumran, in November of 1946, when Jum'a noticed a hole in the rocks so small that it would have been difficult for a cat to enter. Jum'a threw a stone into the hole, and to his astonishment he heard a clink like the breaking of pottery. Jum'a also observed a larger hole a little higher than the small one that was of sufficient size for a person to enter. Jum'a told his cousins Muhammad and Khalil about the holes, but the sun was setting, and they decided to postpone an exploration of the cave to another day. The three cousins agreed to explore the cave together in hope of finding gold or some other treasure.

But Muhammad Ahmed el-Hamed couldn't wait. The day after Jum'a made the discovery, the three cousins had to take their sheep and goats a short way off for water, and afterward returned to their camp near Khirbat Qumran. Shortly after sunrise two days after the original discovery, while

A little to the left of center are the openings to Cave I, where the original Dead Sea Scrolls were discovered; Cave II, where more of the scrolls were found, is at the upper left.

his two cousins were still asleep near their flocks, Muhammad slipped off and climbed up to the cave, three hundred feet from where they were camping. He was able to ease himself feet-first through the larger opening and slide down to the cave floor.

Once his eyes adjusted to the darkness, Muhammad saw ten tall jars along the walls of the cave. In one of the jars, he discovered several old scrolls with writing on them. When he showed the scrolls to his two cousins, they were angry that he had broken their agreement to explore the cave together. His cousins soon forgave Muhammad, and they seem to have agreed to try and sell the old scrolls and share the proceeds.

Partly because it seems unlikely that Muhammad would keep what appeared to be valuable scrolls in a skin bag for "more than two years," the second version of the story seems closer to the truth. However, scholars now believe that Muhammad discovered the scrolls in 1947, when he was around fifteen years old, rather than in 1946. It is understandable that in his first version Muhammad omitted the information about his two cousins' involvement. He must have felt ashamed to tell interviewers that he broke his agreement with his cousins and explored the cave alone.

Each Saturday, farmers' market day attracted large numbers of Taamirah Bedouins to Bethlehem. One Saturday at least two of the cousins hid the scrolls in blankets and accompanied their tribe to Bethlehem. While their friends and relatives sold milk and cheese and purchased items in the market, the cousins entered an antique shop. The antiques dealer thought the scrolls were just fifty- or one-hundred-year-old Jewish manuscripts of little value. Eventually, however, the cousins sold the scrolls. This began a period during which the scrolls were owned by several collectors and shown to a small number of people.

One reason the scrolls secretly passed from hand to hand was that the region was in turmoil, much as it had been two thousand years earlier at the time of the Roman invasion. In 1920 Great Britain took control of a large region called Palestine. Then in 1947—the year the scrolls were probably discovered—the United Nations agreed to create a Jewish homeland out of part of Palestine. This Jewish nation, Israel, was officially born in 1948. Many Arabs in the region did not recognize Israel's existence. War broke out between the new country and its Arab neighbors. The fighting has continued to this day.

However, in the late 1940s, the region where the scrolls were found was not controlled by Israel but by the Arab country of Jordan. Having been found on land belonging to Jordan, the scrolls might be claimed by Jordanian authorities. Israel would also want the scrolls, which were written by Jews for Jewish readers. Perhaps even Britain, which was just giving up control of the region, would want the scrolls. Out of fear that the scrolls would be seized by one government or another, everyone who owned them was rather secretive about it.

The scrolls weren't just one century or even a few centuries old. They were approximately *two thousand years old.*

During this period biblical scholar John C. Trever was asked to determine how old the scrolls might be. In 1948 Dr. Trever, who was then working in Jerusalem, became the first American to examine and photograph the ancient documents. He and other biblical scholars came to a startling conclusion. The scrolls weren't just one century or even a few centuries old. They were approximately *two thousand years old*—making them the oldest biblical manuscripts ever discovered. Muhammad Ahmed el-Hamed had made what was hailed as one of the greatest discoveries of the twentieth century.

In the late 1940s and the 1950s, Bedouins and archaeologists discovered hundreds of additional ancient scrolls in caves near where Muhammad made the original discovery. Because the documents were all found near the Dead Sea, they became known as the Dead Sea Scrolls. One of the oldest of the Dead Sea Scrolls, a fragment of the Book of Exodus, dates from about 250 B.C. It and some other very early Dead Sea Scrolls were apparently not copied by the Essenes at Khirbat Qumran but were brought there as part of a still earlier library. Several of the Dead Sea Scrolls, including the Book of Daniel, were copied by the Essenes just a few years after they were originally written. Another fascinating aspect of the Dead Sea Scrolls is that the wording in them is similar to modern versions of the Old Testament. This shows that the Bible has been faithfully copied and translated over the ages.

Today the major Dead Sea Scrolls are owned by Israel. They are housed in a sanctuary called the Shrine of the Book at the Israel Museum in Jerusalem. Their original discoverer, Muhammad Ahmed el-Hamed, later married, became the father of five daughters, and made his home in Amman, Jordan.

Dr. John C. Trever (left) studying the Dead Sea Scrolls with a religious leader in Jerusalem.

Cave IV, another cave where Dead Sea Scrolls were found, including the Book of Exodus fragment dating from about 250 B.C.

XI Jocelyn Bell

The Discovery of Pulsars

In 1967, Jocelyn Bell, a twenty-four-year-old student working with a radio telescope in England, discovered a weird source of radio signals in the sky. The incredible thing about the radio pulses was that they came at a regular interval—every one and a third seconds. Jocelyn considered the possibilities. Because of the regularity of the signals, it was conceivable that they were being sent out by extraterrestrials who were trying to let us know they were there. Another possibility was that the signals were emanating from a very strange and previously unknown type of heavenly body.

Susan Jocelyn Bell was born on July 15, 1943, in Belfast, the capital of the little country of Northern Ireland. Her family was well-off financially. Jocelyn, as she was called, grew up on an estate called Solitude in a rather remote area of Northern Ireland. Jocelyn had few friends nearby, so as a child she played with her two younger sisters and younger brother, or she amused herself. She later told interviewers that one of her favorite childhood activities was building automobiles and homes for her dolls with her toy construction set.

The Bells were Quakers, a religious group that strongly opposes war and stresses the uniqueness and equality of all people. Also called the Religious Society of Friends, the Quakers advocated equality for blacks and women at times when other faiths were silent on these issues. The Quakers are also known for allowing anyone who feels moved by God to speak out at their "meetings for worship," as they call their religious gatherings. Jocelyn Bell later said that her Quaker heritage encouraged her to think for herself and to have the confidence to present her views.

Bell later said that her Quaker heritage encouraged her to think for herself and to have the confidence to present her views.

Jocelyn's father was a noted architect who designed, among other structures, an addition to Northern Ireland's Armagh Observatory. Jocelyn's father took her to this observatory, where she met professional astronomers, when she was still a child. Jocelyn began reading every astronomy book she could find and decided to become an astronomer when she grew up. Two things stood in her way. The country school she attended was not first-rate. And when she was eleven years old, she flunked an important school examination given at that time. This meant that she could only continue at a public school that would prepare her for vocational work rather than a college-preparatory school. Only by attending a private school could she fulfill her dream of going to college and becoming an astronomer.

Fortunately, her family had the means and the desire to send Jocelyn to a private school. At thirteen, she went to England, where she enrolled at a Quaker boarding school for girls in the city of York. Jocelyn did very well during her six years at the Mount School. She graduated in 1961 at the age of eighteen, then entered the University of Glasgow in Scotland, where she studied physics. Following her graduation from the University of Glasgow in 1965, she was accepted as a doctoral student by the radio astronomy group at Cambridge University, the school where Isaac Newton had studied and later taught.

Modern astronomers don't just *look* at heavenly bodies, for the light our eyes see is only one part of what is called the electromagnetic spectrum. Other portions of the spectrum—ultraviolet rays, X-rays, gamma rays, infrared rays, and radio waves—are invisible to our eyes. With special instruments, astronomers can study these rays and waves produced by heavenly bodies. The study of heavenly bodies by means of analyzing their radio waves is called radio astronomy. Scientists who do these studies are called radio astronomers, and the instruments they employ are called radio telescopes.

Although radio telescopes are nicknamed the "ears of astronomy," radio astronomers don't actually listen with these instruments. The radio signals, which resemble radio static, can be recorded as wavy lines on a chart, and in some cases are converted into a picture.

One advantage of radio telescopes is that they can locate objects that don't emit enough light to be visible in optical telescopes. They can also be used around the clock and at times when optical telescopes are of little use. Radio waves travel through clouds. Daylight doesn't interfere with them, either; though our sun's glare makes most celestial objects invisible to our eyes during daytime, the heavenly bodies are still out there, emitting signals that radio telescopes can monitor.

In the 1950s, radio astronomers discovered a number of distant sources emitting powerful radio signals. Using the 200-inch Mount Palomar Observatory telescope in California, astronomers visually located the sources of some of these signals. They learned that each of the objects generating these strong signals resembled an ordinary star but emitted more energy than an entire typical galaxy. (A galaxy is a group of millions of stars, such as our Milky Way Galaxy, moving together through space.) These objects were named *quasi-stellar radio sources*, meaning starlike radio sources. They are known as *quasars* for short.

Quasars are among the most distant objects yet discovered. So vast are astronomical distances that astronomers measure them in a unit called the light-year, which is equal to about 5,880,000,000,000 (5.88 trillion) miles. Some quasars were found to be located ten billion light-years from us, which equals about 50,880,000, 000,000,000,000,000 (fifty sextillion, eight hundred and eighty quintillion) miles. To put that in perspective, if you made a model of the universe and used a scale in which Earth and the sun, which are actually ninety-three million miles apart, were just a foot apart, a quasar ten billion light-years away would have to be placed a hundred billion miles from the model sun. Simply stated, quasars are so far away the distances can make your head swim!

Graduate students like Bell were half-jokingly known as "slave labor," because they were expected to do much of the busy work.

Jocelyn Bell arrived at Cambridge University in 1965 to work for her doctorate degree under radio astronomer Antony Hewish's supervision. At this time Hewish was preparing to construct a big radio telescope with which to identify quasars. Around universities, graduate students like Bell were half-jokingly known as "slave labor," because they were expected to do much of the busy work for their supervising professors. For her first two years at Cambridge, Bell helped build the radio telescope for Professor Hewish's quasar investigation. Although small in size, Jocelyn learned to swing a twenty-pound sledgehammer. By the time the radio telescope was completed, it had more than two thousand antennas, 120 miles of wire, and covered four and a half acres. Because of that, it became known as the "four and a half acre radio telescope."

In July of 1967—around the time of Jocelyn's twenty-fourth birthday—the radio telescope went into service. Impressed by Bell's ability, Professor Hewish assigned her the crucial jobs of operating the radio telescope and analyzing the data.

As the instrument scanned the sky, the radio signals coming in were recorded in the form of squiggly lines on chart paper. About a hundred feet of chart paper covered with data was produced each day. A computer might have been able to analyze all this data, but, as Bell explained in an article she wrote for *Sky and Telescope* magazine in 1978: "We agreed that the charts should be analyzed by hand, because with a new instrument the output should be scrutinized carefully to make sure that all is operating properly."

Jocelyn Bell at the "four and a half acre radio telescope," which she helped build and where she made her great discovery.

It proved to be a wise decision to analyze the information by hand. "The computer could not have been explicitly programmed to look for unexpected phenomena," Bell explained. And it was "unexpected phenomena" that made the project so noteworthy.

"I struggled to keep up with the paper spewing out of the pen recorders" of the radio telescope, continued Bell. The four and a half acre radio telescope needed four days to make one complete scan of the sky. This meant that Bell had about four hundred feet of chart paper to study for each complete sky survey, eight hundred feet of paper to analyze over an eight-day period, and three thousand feet, or more than half a mile, of chart paper to scrutinize each month.

The "patch of scruff" observed by Bell in October of 1967 would prove to be a major astronomical discovery.

Like a doctor studying a patient's electrocardiogram (a printed record of a heart test), Bell had to separate important signals from those of no significance. She spent a lot of time differentiating signals from space from those generated by such man-made sources as television and radio stations, aircraft equipment, and even automobile ignitions.

After several weeks of analyzing the charts, Jocelyn Bell became aware of an odd radio source in a certain part of the sky. It wasn't a quasar, nor did it look like man-made interference. Recorded on the chart paper, this odd signal looked like "a patch of scruff," wrote Bell. "Scruff" is an English expression referring to something worthless or untidy, but the "patch of scruff" observed by Bell in October of 1967 would prove to be a major astronomical discovery.

"I began to remember that I had seen this particular bit of scruff before, and from the same part of the sky," Jocelyn Bell later told *Science* magazine. "This bit of scruff was something I didn't completely understand—my brain just hung on to it and I remembered I had seen it before." Reviewing her charts, she found that the "patch of scruff" was first recorded in August.

She told Professor Hewish about the unusual radio source, and together they agreed that it merited additional study. Because some tests on a quasar had to be completed first, Bell couldn't turn her attention to the mystery object for a few weeks. Then, on November 28, she came across the "patch of scruff" again. Writing in *Sky and Telescope*, she described what occurred on that Tuesday:

> *As the chart flowed I saw the pen trace a series of pulses. They were not all the same height, but they did seem to be equally spaced. When the "source" had passed I took the chart off the recorder and checked; the pulses were equally spaced, at one and a third seconds.*

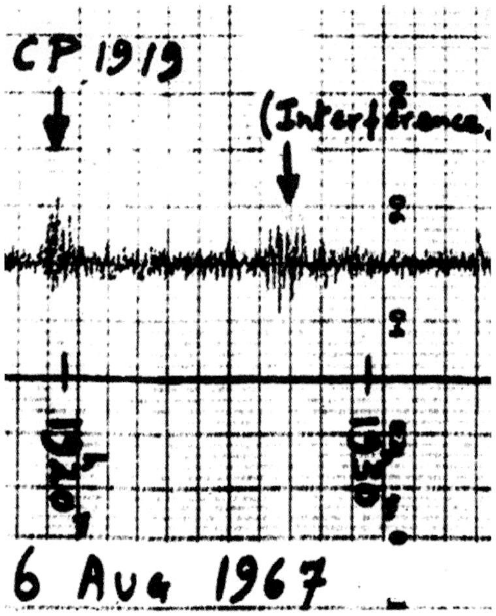

Chart showing the first appearance of the "patch of scruff" from CP 1919, the first pulsar ever discovered; at right is radio interference, which could be difficult to differentiate from pulsar signals.

Bell phoned Hewish and told him about the regular pulses that came at intervals of a second and one-third. "That settles it—it must be man-made," he commented. The signals had to be coming from something on Earth, he believed, because as of 1967 no known celestial objects sent out pulses so regularly and so rapidly. Further research by Hewish's colleagues revealed that the pulses came with amazing regularity: every 1.3373011 seconds. The intervals between the pulses were consistent to within a *millionth* of a second.

There was a way for Jocelyn Bell to tell whether the signals were from a star or from some human transmission on Earth. People keep time according to a twenty-four-hour day. But the astronomical day is a bit shorter. Each night any given star rises about four minutes earlier than it did the night before, so the astronomical day consists of about twenty-three hours and fifty-six minutes. People sometimes call this astronomical day "star time." Bell timed when the mystery signals reappeared each day. If they reappeared at twenty-four-hour intervals, then they probably resulted from some kind of man-made radio interference based on Earth. But if the pulses occurred four minutes earlier each night, they were coming from deep space.

The signals appeared four minutes earlier per day. They truly were coming from the realm of the stars. But that just placed Bell and Hewish back at square one. It seemed beyond belief that a natural object could produce signals with such regularity and with such short intervals between them.

At this point Bell and Hewish began to consider another possibility. The signals might not be *man*-made, yet they might have been produced by intelligent creatures anyway. Perhaps they were messages beamed into space by extraterrestrials living on a planet far beyond our solar system.

That possibility was not so far-fetched. It we ever make contact with extraterrestrials, it may be via messages received by radio telescopes. The vast distances in space make it unlikely that we will ever make a trip by rocket to planetary systems beyond our sun's family of planets. As mentioned earlier, the star nearest the sun, Proxima Centauri, is 4.3 light-years, or about 25 trillion miles, from us. Even if we could build rocket ships that could go 250,000 miles per hour, it would take more than 10,000 years to reach Proxima Centauri. Other stars are hundreds or even millions of times farther from us than that.

But, assuming extraterrestrials are out there, we might be able to communicate with them without leaving home. FM radio as well as TV signals travel forever into space at the speed of light—186,282 miles per second. Each year an FM radio or TV signal travels one light-year through space. After twenty years the signal will have traveled twenty light-years, and after a century it will have traveled a hundred light-years. Imagine that in the year 2006 extraterrestrials fifty light-years away aim their radio telescopes at Earth and tune into the proper frequencies. Then they might be able to intercept our radio and TV shows from 1956. If the extraterrestrials built large antenna systems and special receivers, they could actually listen to our radio broadcasts and watch our TV shows. But more likely they would only detect our signals as static, or "scruff" as Jocelyn Bell called it.

Just as ETs might intercept our broadcasts with radio telescopes, we might do the same with theirs. Through further study, it was learned that Jocelyn Bell's mystery object was about 212 light-years from Earth. Perhaps the ETs had sent out broadcasts in what we call the year 1755. Those signals would have zoomed through space, traveling 212 light-years in 212 years, and possibly been intercepted by Jocelyn Bell as "a patch of scruff" in 1967.

"Were there some 'men' out there signaling to us?" Bell wrote in *Sky and*

Telescope. "Was that why the signals appeared man-made but moved like a star?"

Good scientists don't discount any rational possibility, yet the prospect of extraterrestrials sending out broadcasts sounded so weird that Professor Hewish and his colleagues felt a little strange talking about it. Nonetheless, Jocelyn Bell coined a name for the tentative possibility that extraterrestrials sent the signals. She called it the LGM (for Little Green Men) hypothesis.

Bell coined a name for the tentative possibility that extraterrestrials sent the signals. She called it the LGM (for Little Green Men) hypothesis.

One evening shortly before Christmas, Jocelyn Bell entered Professor Hewish's office to talk to him and found that she was intruding on a high-level conference of radio astronomers discussing how to announce the discovery of this unusual signal. "We did not really believe it was little green men," Bell later recalled about this period, "but on the other hand we had no proof that it was not, nor had we any convincing alternatives to suggest."

Bell was about to leave Cambridge and return home for her Christmas holiday, but she had about a third of a mile's worth of charts yet to be analyzed. So, following the meeting about LGM in Professor Hewish's office, Jocelyn ate supper, then returned to the radio telescope lab to do some chart work.

While studying the charts, as she later recounted in *Sky and Telescope*, she found another signal that "looked remarkably like scruff—only this time it was from a different part of the sky." Searching through old charts, she found several other occasions when this second patch of scruff had been recorded.

Wanting to check further on this second odd radio source, late that night she went out to the radio telescope, which was located near the university. It was so cold that the instrument wouldn't work properly. "I breathed hot air on it, I kicked and swore at it, and I got it to work for just five minutes. It was the right five minutes," she told *Science* magazine. During that time the instrument recorded a series of pulses from the second source. Incredibly, they were even more rapid than the first source, occurring at intervals of about one and a quarter seconds.

Bell left the charts for the second source on Professor Hewish's desk, then went home for the holidays. Upon her return to Cambridge in January of 1968, she found two more of these odd radio sources, one of which pulsed every quarter of a second. With four similar fast-pulsing sources in the sky, the LGM theory was ruled out. The chances of intercepting signals

Jocelyn Bell at about the time she discovered pulsars.

from *one* extraterrestrial civilization were extremely slim. Finding similar signals from *four* different civilizations within several months would be virtually impossible. The pulses were undoubtedly some type of natural phenomenon from heavenly bodies.

The Cambridge University radio astronomy team couldn't decide whether to call the objects sending out regular signals "pulsating radio stars" or "pulsed radio stars." In 2003 Jocelyn Bell informed me how they received their name. One day in 1968, she explained, the science correspondent for the British newspaper the *Daily Telegraph* wrote the name *pulsar* on a blackboard at Cambridge. That name for the stars stuck.

[Pulsars] proved to be among the most unusual objects in the universe.

Antony Hewish and his radio astronomy team quickly wrote an article announcing the discovery of pulsars. Hewish, Bell, and three other radio astronomers involved in the study of these objects were listed as the authors of the article, which appeared in the British journal *Nature* in February of 1968.

By late 1968, astronomers knew the basic facts about pulsars, which proved to be among the most unusual objects in the universe. Like everything else, stars don't last forever. Our sun, for example, has been shining for about 4.6 billion years and, according to astronomers, will continue to do so for another 5 billion years. Then it will begin the dying process that will eventually turn it into a cold, burned-out object called a black dwarf. Our middle-aged sun is a medium-size star. Some larger stars go through a different dying process. They collapse, causing a gargantuan explosion called a supernova, which propels huge amounts of star material into space. What is left behind is a neutron star, which, despite being only several miles across, is so dense that a thimbleful of its material would weigh hundreds of millions of tons. Pulsars are a kind of neutron star.

Besides being incredibly dense, pulsars spin very rapidly, typically about two times per second. As it spins, a pulsar emits a beam of radio waves that can sometimes be detected by our radio telescopes.

Investigations of pulsars helped us understand the life of stars. Along with such phenomena as quasars and black holes, pulsars also showed that the universe is a far more intriguing place than astronomers once thought. For these reasons, the discovery of pulsars was an important event in the history of astronomy.

Pulsars showed that the universe is a far more intriguing place than astronomers once thought.

For a while, Jocelyn Bell was a media favorite as journalists visited Cambridge to photograph and interview her. But by the end of 1969 she had received her doctorate, gotten married, and left radio astronomy. Over the next few years she taught astronomy, had a son, and did volunteer work for Quaker causes.

Astronomers are sometimes pictured as absentminded people who don't care for earthly things. The truth is, they like to be recognized for their work the same as anyone else. In 1973 the Franklin Institute of Philadelphia, Pennsylvania, awarded its prestigious Albert A. Michelson medal jointly to Jocelyn Bell and Antony Hewish. Bell won for discovering pulsars, and Hewish for directing the project in which Bell worked. Bell also won several other major prizes for discovering pulsars.

To most people, though, the Nobel Prizes are the greatest scientific awards. The 1974 Nobel Prize for Physics was awarded jointly to two radio astronomers: Antony Hewish, for the discovery of pulsars, and Cambridge radio astronomer Martin Ryle, under whom Hewish had worked. Jocelyn Bell was not included.

The Nobel Prize committee had concluded that the discovery was

Hewish's because Jocelyn Bell just carried out his instructions. Hewish agreed. "Jocelyn was a jolly good girl but she was just doing her job," he told *Science* magazine. "She noticed this source was doing this thing. If she hadn't noticed it, it would have been negligent."

Some prominent scientists thought that Bell received a raw deal. The great prize was "pinched from the girl," meaning stolen, famed British astronomer Fred Hoyle asserted. Astronomer Thomas Gold argued that Hewish had assigned Bell to study quasars. She serendipitously discovered a completely different type of object—pulsars. So how could it be said that she was only following Hewish's program? Besides, the discovery was not as easily achieved as Hewish implied. At least one other astronomer in Britain had found pulsar signals on his charts but figured they were so strange they couldn't possibly be coming from a star.

Writing in the August 1, 1975, *Science* magazine, Nicholas Wade pointed out that Bell had done everything expected of a discoverer. She had noticed unusual radio signals, made certain they were keeping star time so that they couldn't be coming from Earth, searched through old records to verify the discovery, then found similar signals in other parts of the sky to prove that they were a new kind of natural phenomenon. Wade also countered the argument, made by some people, that if Bell hadn't discovered pulsars, the next graduate student working for Hewish would have.

"With this 'what if' argument," wrote Wade, "almost every scientist could be stripped of his credit, in that every discovery would have been made by somebody else sooner or later. The historical fact is that it was Burnell [Jocelyn Bell's married name], and not another individual, who discovered the pulsar signals."

Jocelyn Bell did not show any bitterness about being deprived of the Nobel Prize. For her, it was enough that as a twenty-four-year-old graduate student she had been involved in a great discovery. At the end of her March 1978 *Sky and Telescope* article, Jocelyn Bell Burnell wrote:

> *The discovery could not have been accomplished without a lot of luck and hard work. In return it has brought me enormous enjoyment, some undeserved fame, and opportunities to get to know many interesting people—marvelous rewards in themselves.*

In 2001 Jocelyn Bell Burnell became dean of science at England's University of Bath, where she helped prepare a new generation of young people for a fresh century of discovery.

Afterword

A Note to Future Discoverers

Discoveries are still being made—often thanks to some unexpected good fortune. One of the greatest discoveries of the 1990s was helped along by a little serendipity.

People have long wondered: Are stars other than the sun orbited by planets? The question has intriguing ramifications. Stars are too hot for living things, but planets can support life, as our Earth proves. If stars commonly have planets, then life in the universe is probably abundant. But if planets are rare, we could be alone. By the late 1980s scientists believed that planets were plentiful, yet they had not found any beyond our own solar system.

In 1990 radio astronomer Alex Wolszczan (VOL-shtan) was working in Puerto Rico at Arecibo Observatory, operated by Cornell University. The observatory's 1,000-foot-diameter radio telescope was broken and required repairs. "All you could do was park it in certain positions for brief periods of time," Dr. Wolszczan recalls. For Wolszczan, who had been born in Poland in 1946, this proved to be the break of a lifetime.

Because of the repairs, the giant radio telescope was closed to visiting astronomers, but Dr. Wolszczan, as a staff member, was free to use it. He decided to search for millisecond pulsars. Unlike the pulsars first discovered by Jocelyn Bell, which typically rotate roughly twice per second, millisecond pulsars complete one spin in only several *thousandths* of a second.

In early 1990 Dr. Wolszczan discovered a new millisecond pulsar rotating an amazing 161 times per second. Millisecond pulsars send out radio pulses so regularly that "they keep time comparably to the most accurate clocks ever built—atomic clocks," Dr. Wolszczan explains. But there was something strange about this pulsar, which was named PSR 1257+12 for its position in the sky. Sometimes its pulses arrived a little

One of the world's great astronomical instruments, the 1,000-foot-diameter Arecibo Radio Telescope in Puerto Rico, where Alex Wolszczan discovered the first extrasolar planets.

early and sometimes they arrived a little late. Millisecond pulsars don't behave like that! Dr. Wolszczan told himself.

Returning to Cornell University in Ithaca, New York, he tackled the mystery. One day in the fall of 1991 Dr. Wolszczan had a revelation similar to that of Isaac Newton about 325 years earlier, only instead of watching an apple, Alex was studying computer data. By chance he had found a very special millisecond pulsar. "I realized there were planets around that star," he recalls. The gravitation of at least two planets tugged PSR 1257+12 sometimes toward and sometimes away from us, causing some of its pulses to reach us a little ahead of schedule, and others to arrive a little tardy.

Wolszczan announced his results in the journal *Nature* in January of 1992. He concluded that PSR 1257+12 has one planet approximately three

Dr. Alex Wolszczan

and a half times the size of Earth and another approximately three Earths in size. Other astronomers verified the results. Although planets were the furthest thing from his mind when he began his millisecond pulsar project, Alex Wolszczan was hailed as the discoverer of the first known extrasolar planets (planets orbiting stars beyond the sun). Since then a number of other planets have been discovered orbiting various stars. It now appears that roughly a quarter of all stars have planets, which implies that life in the universe is probably abundant.

In the future, more momentous discoveries will be made, for major problems and questions in many scientific fields await solution. How can we conquer cancer and AIDS? Is there life on other worlds? What will we use to supply energy when our fossil fuels run out? Can the human life span be greatly extended? What's the best way to repair the damage we have done to Earth's air and water? Can the droughts and other weather extremes that kill many thousands of people each year be prevented? People who are now children may one day solve these problems and answer these questions—with some hard work and perhaps a little boost from serendipity.

Dr. Wolszczan has advice for the discoverers of tomorrow. "Choose work and put yourself in an environment that has potential for discovery." If you hope to make a medical discovery, become a medical researcher like Alexander Fleming. If your dream is to develop a new kind of rocket, enter the aerospace field.

Dr. Wolszczan has something to add:

> *With a discovery involving serendipity there is always a point when you can either overlook something or you can catch it and try to study it further. In my case, I could have said I'll worry about [the oddities of PSR 1257+12] later and gone on with something else. I didn't do that. I followed up on it.*

Having been in research many years, I have seen many discoveries people could have made but missed because they didn't pay attention to unusual phenomena. In fact, some people get so involved in routine that they actually get annoyed *when things don't work as expected. To young people, I would say don't get enslaved by routine because if you turn off your brain you will not notice out-of-the-ordinary phenomena. Keep your eyes wide open for something unusual at all times.*

Bibliographical Sources

i Isaac Newton: The Fall of an Apple

When I was thirteen, my father's friend Maxim Hirsch gave me his personal underlined copy of *And There Was Light* by Rudolf Thiel (Knopf, 1957). This book, which I have treasured for nearly half a century, was of great help for this chapter. Other books consulted: *The World of Copernicus* by Angus Armitage (Signet, 1963); *Memoirs of the Life, Writings, and Discoveries of Sir Isaac Newton*, vol. 1, by Sir David Brewster (Constable, 1855); *Isaac Newton and the Scientific Revolution* by Gale Christianson (Oxford, 1996); and *Sir Isaac Newton* by E. N. da C. Andrade (Doubleday, 1954).

ii Mary Anning: "The Princess of Paleontology"

The main resources for this chapter were articles by W. D. Lang in the English journal *Proceedings of the Dorset Natural History and Archaeological Society*: "Mary Anning and the Pioneer Geologists of Lyme" (vol. 60, 1939, pp. 142–164); "Three Letters by Mary Anning, 'Fossilist,' of Lyme" (vol. 66, 1945, pp. 169–173); "More about Mary Anning, Including a Newly-Found Letter" (vol. 71, 1950, pp. 184–188); "Mary Anning and the Fire at Lyme in 1844" (vol. 74, 1953, pp. 175–177); "Mary Anning and Anna Maria Pinney" (vol. 76, 1956, pp. 146–152); "Mary Anning's Escape from Lightning" (vol. 80, 1959, pp. 91–93); and "Portraits of Mary Anning and Other Items" (vol. 81, 1960, pp. 89–91). Another helpful Lang article was "Mary Anning of Lyme, Collector and Vendor of Fossils, 1799–1847," from the British *Natural History Magazine* (vol. 5, 1935, pp. 64–81). Books consulted: *Curious Bones: Mary Anning and the Birth of Paleontology* by Thomas Goodhue (Morgan Reynolds, 2002); *Reading Between the Bones: The Pioneers of Dinosaur Paleontology* by Susan Clinton (Franklin Watts, 1997); and *Before the Deluge* by Herbert Wendt (Doubleday, 1968).

iii Charles Goodyear: "The Rubber Man"

Information for this chapter came from biographies of Goodyear: *The Goodyear Story* by Richard Korman (Encounter Books, 2002); *Trials of an Inventor: Life and Discoveries of Charles Goodyear* by Bradford Peirce (Phillips and Hunt, 1866); and *India Rubber Man: The Story of Charles Goodyear* by Ralph Wolf (Caxton, 1939).

iv Anesthesia: "The Greatest Discovery Ever Made"

A few years ago in connection with my book *We Have Conquered Pain*, I visited museums and historic sites in Georgia, Massachusetts, and Connecticut associated with the discovery of anesthesia. Helpful books consulted: *The First Anesthetic: The Story of Crawford Long* by Frank Boland (University of Georgia, 1950); *Horace Wells, Dentist: Father of Surgical Anesthesia,* edited by William Gies (Horace Wells Centenary Committee, 1948); *Victory over Pain: Morton's Discovery of Anesthesia* by Betty MacQuitty (Taplinger, 1971); *The Gift of Magic Sleep: Early Experiments in Anesthesia* by Irwin Shapiro (Coward, McCann & Geoghegan, 1979); and *I Awaken to Glory,* edited by Richard Wolfe and Leonard Menczer (Boston Medical Library, 1994).

v Ignaz Semmelweis: Doctors, Wash Your Hands!

I consulted several books about my medical hero, Ignaz Semmelweis. The most helpful: *Childbed Fever: A Scientific Biography of Ignaz Semmelweis* by K. Codell Carter and Barbara R. Carter (Greenwood Press, 1994); *Semmelweis: His Life and Work* by Gyorgy Gortvay and Imre Zoltan (published in Budapest, Hungary, in 1968); *Semmelweis: His Life and His Doctrine* by Sir William Sinclair (University of Manchester Press, 1909); and *Immortal Magyar: Semmelweis, Conquerer of Childbed Fever* by Frank Slaughter (Schuman, 1950).

vi Maria Sanz de Sautuola: The Bulls on the Ceiling

In 1985–1986, Maria's son Emilio Botin wrote me several letters relating details about Maria's life. He also gave me *Escritos y Documentos de Marcelino Sanz de Sautuola* [*Writings and Documents of Marcelino Sanz de Sautuola*] (published in Santander, Spain, in 1976). With the aid of a Spanish-English dictionary, this book was of great help.

vii Alexander Fleming: Discoverer of Penicillin

The bulk of the information for this chapter came from two sources: *Alexander Fleming: The Man and the Myth* by Gwyn Macfarlane (Harvard, 1984); and *The Life of Sir Alexander Fleming: Discoverer of Penicillin* by André Maurois (Dutton, 1959).

viii Clyde Tombaugh: The Search for Planet X

Clyde provided me with much information during a visit we had at his New Mexico home in late 1995. In 1996 Venetia Burney Phair wrote me a letter explaining how as a child she suggested the name Pluto for the ninth planet. Books consulted were: *Out of the Darkness: The Planet Pluto* by Clyde Tombaugh and Patrick Moore (Stackpole Books, 1980); *Clyde Tombaugh: Discoverer of Planet Pluto* by David H. Levy (University of Arizona Press, 1991); and *Planets Beyond: Discovering the Outer Solar System* by Mark Littmann (Wiley, 1988).

ix Lise Meitner: The Discovery of Nuclear Fission

Three books provided much of the information for this chapter: *Lise Meitner: A Life in Physics* by Ruth Lewin Sime (University of California Press, 1996); *Otto Hahn and the Rise of Nuclear Physics,* edited by William Shea (published in Dordrecht, the Netherlands, in 1983); and *Nobel Prize Women in Science* by Sharon Bertsch McGrayne (Birch Lane Press, 1993). Articles consulted: "Looking Back" by Lise Meitner in the November 1964 *Bulletin of the Atomic Scientists* (pp. 2–7); and "Is the Atom Terror Exaggerated?" by George Axelsson in the January 5, 1946, *Saturday Evening Post* (pp. 34–50).

x Muhammad Ahmed el-Hamed: The Dead Sea Scrolls

In 1986, Dr. John C. Trever, the first American scholar to study and photograph the

Dead Sea Scrolls, wrote me several letters about Muhammad Ahmed el-Hamed. Books consulted: *The Untold Story of Qumran* by John C. Trever (Revell, 1965); *The People of the Dead Sea Scrolls* by John Marco Allegro (Doubleday, 1958); and *The Bedouin* by Shirley Kay (Crane, Russak, 1978). Articles consulted: "Muhammad Ed-Deeb's Own Story of His Scroll Discovery" by William Brownlee in the October 1957 *Journal of Near Eastern Studies* (vol. 16, no. 4, pp. 236–239); "Edh-Dheeb's Story of His Scroll Discovery" by William Brownlee in the October 1962 *Revue de Qumran* (pp. 483–494); and "When Was Qumran Cave One Discovered?" by John C. Trever in the February 1961 *Revue de Qumran* (pp. 135–141).

xi Jocelyn Bell: The Discovery of Pulsars

The book *Nobel Prize Women in Science* by Sharon Bertsch McGrayne (Birch Lane Press, 1993) was of great help for this chapter. Of additional help were the articles "Little Green Men, White Dwarfs, or What?" by S. Jocelyn Bell Burnell in the March 1978 *Sky and Telescope* (pp. 218–221); and "Discovery of Pulsars: A Graduate Student's Story" by Nicholas Wade in the August 1, 1975, *Science* (pp. 358–364). Jocelyn Bell Burnell was kind enough to read this chapter and make several suggestions.

Afterword: A Note to Future Discoverers

The information for the afterword came from interviews I conducted with Dr. Alex Wolszczan in 1996 and 2003.

Picture Credits

Arecibo Observatory: page 174

Emilio Botin: pages 89, 95

Jocelyn Bell Burnell: pages 162, 168

Churchill College Archives Centre, Cambridge: pages 133, 135, 145

Czeslaw Czaplinski © 2005: page 175

Judith Bloom Fradin: pages 4, 9, 22, 35

The Goodyear Tire & Rubber Company: pages 42, 45

David Gregory & Debbie Marshall/Wellcome Photo Library: page 99

International Museum of Surgical Science, Chicago, Illinois: pages 68, 86

Library of Congress: pages 49, 105

Lowell Observatory Archives: pages 124, 126, 127

Lyme Regis Museum: page 27

Massachusetts General Hospital, Archives and Special Collections: page 63

Mullard Radio Astronomy Observatory: page 164

National Library of Medicine: pages 52, 55, 59, 61, 65, 74

The Natural History Museum, London: pages 19, 25, 26

North Wind Picture Archives: pages 15, 31, 92, 103

Pfizer Inc.: page 81

Venetia Burney Phair: page 128

Stock Montage, Inc.: pages 13, 71, 131, 144

Mrs. Clyde W. Tombaugh and the New Mexico State University Library, Archives and Special Collections: page 122

John C. Trever: pages 150, 153, 156, 157

Wellcome Photo Library: pages 109, 112